S.W.A.T

SEEKING WISDOM AND TRUTH

JON ZIRPOLO

SWAT: Seeking Wisdom and Truth

Copyright © 2026

Published by Kaio Publications, Inc.
kaiopublications.org

All rights reserved. No portion of this book may be reproduced in any form without the written permission of the author or publisher, including translation.

Unless otherwise noted, all Scripture is taken from the New King James Version®. Copyright © 1982 by Thomas Nelson. Used by permission. All rights reserved.

ISBN: 978-1-952955-57-0

 Dedication

I dedicate this book:

To the God from whom all blessings flow…

To my wife who has always been a light in my darkest hours…

To my kids who love me even when I fail…

    And to you…

    The one who just needs encouragement,

    The one who is struggling,

    The one whose faith has been shaken,

    The one who is thinking of walking away from the church,

    The one who has failed,

    The one who has doubts,

    The one who is searching for answers…

This book is for you.

Table of Contents

Introduction 1
Chapter 1   The Crash that Started It All.....................5
Chapter 2   Alone in the Swamp......................... 11
Chapter 3   The Lambo....................................... 21
Chapter 4   Remember What Judas Forgot..................27
Chapter 5   I've Got a Mansion............................. 33
Chapter 6   Feed My Sheep................................. 39
Chapter 7   When Sheep Turn into Wolves 45
Chapter 8   Checking for Prints............................53
Chapter 9   "Why You Running?"........................63
Chapter 10 Walking with Milan............................71
Chapter 11 Four Things I Remember.......................81
Chapter 12 Life Is Like That Sometimes...................91
Chapter 13 Finding Contentment..........................99
Chapter 14 When the Waves Come.......................107
Chapter 15 SWAT School...................................115

Introduction

It is 0800 hours, October 5, 2012. I'm three hours away from home, standing on a firing line facing my targets: two silhouettes 25 yards away. There are 10 guys standing to my left, 9 more standing to my right, and 15 more waiting their turn. We're all here fighting for a spot that isn't guaranteed to anyone. Standing right behind me is an instructor who is so close, I can smell what kind of toothpaste he used. He's watching with eagle eyes to make sure I shoot when and where I'm supposed to shoot. Sending a bullet to the body when it was supposed to go to the head—doesn't count. Shooting after the timer goes off—doesn't count. There's no cheating on this course.

For the last three months, I had been practicing several times a week at our range. I shot and shot and shot. When I was tired of shooting, I shot more. I sent thousands of bullets down range. I practiced drawing repeatedly just trying to shave a few milliseconds off my time, because those few milliseconds might be the difference maker. I wore out my magazine release doing reload drills. I watched hours (yes…hours) of YouTube videos of professional shooters training and ingested every tip I could to make myself a little better. Failure wasn't an option—I only had one chance.

I triple checked my magazine count, then I checked it again. If you had the wrong number of bullets, you failed. Six rounds loaded into the pistol—check! Two spare magazines with twelve rounds each—check! Safety glasses clean—check! Hearing protection working properly—check! Ready to lose my breakfast? You betcha!

Standing there waiting for the buzzer to sound off, the last three months replayed through my head. Should I have shot a few more rounds? Ran the reload drills a few more times? Ate that extra chocolate glazed donut from Dunkin'? Those things slap...

Then I heard it. The sound to unleash freedom at 1000 feet per second. I drop the safety latch and bypass the trigger guard lock. My grip is solid as the pistol comes out. My left hand finishes the grip, and I punch it out. My sights are all aligned on my first target. Slow is smooth and smooth is fast. Five pounds of pressure to the trigger sends the firing pin forward into primer. A miniature explosion of gunpowder sends a .40 caliber lead bullet screaming out of the barrel leaving a small plume of smoke in its wake…

Welcome to SWAT school.

If you aren't a detective and haven't figured it out yet, SWAT is where the title comes from—*Seeking Wisdom and Truth*. If you think about it, the church is not much different than a SWAT team in a spiritual sense. We are to be seekers of wisdom and truth. And we respond to calls for services of all types, don't we? Someone is having doubts about his faith—we encourage him. A family lost a loved one—we love them. A lost soul looking for hope—we teach him. Someone doesn't know where her next meal is coming from, we give it to her. That's what we do!

SWAT bros have an ol' cliché saying, "Either you're SWAT, or you're not." In the church, the same holds true: you're either **S**eeking **W**isdom **a**nd **T**ruth, or you're not. Whether you're on fire for God or one finding it a battle just to get in the pew on Sunday—this is for you. You might have all the Psalms memorized (that would be impressive) or have to Google verses to remember where they are (cough, cough…like me). Either way, this is for you. A new Christian? This is for you. Been a Christian since Acts 2? This is for you too. Under the age of 16? Weeeell, maybe have Mom or Dad read Chapter 1 before you dive into this, and let them decide if it's for you. In this book I discuss some grown folk stuff. Some of these stories will be around suicide, death, alcohol/drug abuse, etc. and may not be appropriate for the younger eyes. As I tell church elders before I speak in their pulpit, these stories can be X-rated, but I try to keep them at a PG level.

SWAT: Seeking Wisdom and Truth takes you through some of my own experiences from over 20 years of police work. We'll cover some of life's harder challenges and obstacles and consider how they connect to biblical lessons. Together we'll learn how to grow closer to Him while simultaneously lending a hand to those around us. It won't be easy. In fact, it'll probably be one of the hardest journeys you (or I, for that matter) will ever go on. After all, you're either SWAT, or you're not…

CH. 1
The Crash that Started It All

It was July 25, 2009, at around 6:30 a.m. on a warm Saturday morning in South Georgia. My usual routine would take me to the interstate where I would try and nab a drunk driver on his way home. But not today—today I elected to go to the morning briefing and hear about what happened during the night. Maybe I would even go to breakfast. Maybe I would just give my car a good cleaning. Who knew?

My sergeant and I were standing in the parking lot of the police department discussing the comings and goings of the police politics when the dispatch call came through the radios. A vehicle was driving north on our interstate, but it was in the southbound lanes. Now our section of interstate is divided not just by a guardrail, but by a large median full of trees. It's this way for more than ten miles. This means that the driver would have either turned around in the middle of the road or he drove down the wrong ramp at the next exit south of us. Either way, it wasn't a call we could hope would just self-correct. I ran to my 2007 Dodge Charger and off I went.

There wasn't a lot of traffic out at that time of the morning, so I had the ability to "pin the ears back" on my car. I was strolling. We had been driving for less than a minute when we heard the tones drop. When first responders say, "tones drop," it means that our dispatchers send a loud, distinct beeping noise across the radio. In some jurisdictions this will mean that a major crime is being reported (a robbery, shooting, etc.). In my jurisdiction, it means that EMS and/or the fire department is being dispatched. After the tones stopped, our dispatcher reported that the vehicle traveling north in the southbound lanes had just collided head on with another vehicle.

It didn't take very long for me to get there, but it felt like an eternity. Traffic on the interstate was starting to back up and the sun was just cresting at the top of the trees. As we got closer, I could see the smoke rising into the sky. We had to take the shoulder of the road to get around the traffic stopped on the roadway. My sergeant and I were the first ones on scene.

It looked like a war zone. Pure chaos. The two vehicles (a van and a small pickup truck) involved were beyond destroyed. I had never seen anything like it. Car parts were scattered over fifty yards. Glass was everywhere. Horns were blaring. All three lanes were blocked. Gas, oil, and coolant were pouring out of the vehicles. There were bystanders standing in the grass while other people were driving through the grass to get around the wreck.

I went to the van while my sergeant went to the truck. I approached the driver's side and looked in the middle window. I saw a young man sitting upright in his chair but in a fetal position. He was bleeding out of his nose, ears, and mouth. His eyes were shut, and he was slightly rocking back and forth. I moved up to the driver but could only see her left arm. Her body had been completely crushed by the steering wheel and dash. Basically, the engine was in her lap. I walked around to check the front passenger. He was semi-conscious. His eyes followed me as I rounded the front bumper. I asked him if he was okay, but he couldn't answer. He stared at me while rocking back and forth. His right forearm was snapped and was just hanging. He would pass away before EMS could get there. I wouldn't find out for a while later, but there were three more people in the van.

I ran back to my sergeant to examine the pickup truck. Beer cans and bottles were everywhere. The driver wasn't wearing his seatbelt. On impact, he had been launched forward into the A-post of his truck (the sides of your windshield) that had buckled into a point upon impact. As the truck came to a rest, the driver was thrown into the back windshield and came to a final rest in the back seat.

Several EMS and fire trucks arrived and began working at the scene. I was with the medics at the van who extricated the young man in the middle seat behind the driver. He was a 19-year-old from Florida. They were traveling from New York to Florida for a wedding. He was wearing a white undershirt, a red and white Polo, a gold chain with a cross, dark blue jeans, and red and white Jordans. They cut the door open, cut his seatbelt off and we slowly removed him from the van. We laid him on the ground where I grabbed his head to hold it still as the medics did their best to keep him alive. As loud as the scene was, to me in that moment, everything went quiet. Everything seemed to stop. I was just staring down at the young man watching blood run down my hands. I remember looking up and meeting the eyes of the medic looking back at me. He just shook his head left and right. The young man had died while I was holding him.

We were at that scene for more than six hours before we were able to open the roadway back up. Then a few hours later, it hit me: If I had done what I normally did on a Saturday morning, I would have been parked a half mile from the crash site when the original call came out. Perhaps I would have been able to stop the guy before he killed himself and three others. Perhaps he would have taken me out instead of that 19-year-old. So many emotions began running over me. What made me go to the office instead of the interstate? How do I even begin processing what I had seen? There hasn't been a July 25 go by where I don't think about that morning.

The day after this accident my wife and I celebrated our first wedding anniversary. What a great way to end our first year of marriage, right? I tried to explain everything to her, but the right words to make her understand didn't come out. She'd been my friend since 8th grade. She'd been my best friend for a couple years. She had only been my wife for 364 days. But over the next few days, she gave me the best idea that would change my life and my faith forever. How could I process what I was going through? She told me to write it down.

I didn't really understand the idea. I wasn't a writer by any means. I hated writing. I barely passed English in high school. All my papers were bombs. I didn't know what a verb was until I took Spanish in 11th grade. Write it down? Does she even know me? But the more we talked about it, the more brilliant the idea became. It wouldn't be easy. It still isn't most of the time. I've delivered several sermons with this accident in them and have never made it through without crying. My wife's idea was simple, yet so powerful—I could either let this accident destroy me internally or I could use it to help others. But could God really take something so messed up, devastating, and horrifying and use it to His glory?

So, this project was born. Romans 15:4 says, "For whatever things were written before were written for our learning, that we through the patience and comfort of the Scriptures might have hope." Essentially, we can look at the happenings in the Old Testament and learn from their experiences. What follows is a similar idea. These are my stories and experiences from more than two decades of police work. From them, we'll make spiritual applications that will hopefully help you in your Christian walk as you seek wisdom and truth.

All the stories are true stories...mostly. Some of the details have been changed or altered. This isn't done to be deceptive or mislead you, but rather to protect those who may be in them. Some will be funny (hopefully), and some will be more on the sad side. I tried to keep them on the shorter side because you might be like me and have the attention span of a squirrel. My wife can read *War and Peace* in one night. It takes me two days to read a food menu. But as my late friend Ken Richbourg once told me, "No one ever complained about a short lesson."

🏋 WORDS TO WEIGH

1. What event, crisis, or struggle might be your "crash that started it all"? How has it affected you spiritually?

2. How have you handled it and what have you learned? What Scriptures were helpful to you?

CH. 2
Alone in the Swamp

Speed enforcement. There is something horrifying about driving down the highway, minding your own business and then seeing ol' Smokey hiding in the tree line waiting for you, the speed racer. Instant panic sets in even if you are driving under the speed limit. Your body goes into don't-get-a-ticket mode, and you subconsciously remove your foot from the gas pedal. You go from driving 10 over the speed limit to 15 under in less than two seconds. Totally not suspicious at all. As you start to pass by him you contemplate making eye contact. *"Maybe I should look. Maybe I shouldn't. If I look at him, I'll look like I'm guilty. If I don't look at him, he'll suspect I'm smuggling drugs. Do I wave? Perhaps I make a not-so-smooth lane change and pretend I didn't see him?"* As you pass by, you make the decision—you look! Whew, he looks like he's sleeping. Crisis averted.

I am usually on the other end of this scenario. I'm Smokey (just thinner and better looking) hiding around the bend waiting on you, the Bandit. If you don't know who Smokey and the Bandit are, Google it.

It was just before sunset one June evening, and here came my Bandit—an older model Toyota Camry screaming around the curve! The radar unit shrieked as I clocked him doing 103 mph in a 70 mph zone! He waved.

Whew doggy! I came out the hole sideways. Traction control was off and I sent dirt and grass flying! Siri, play "Highway to the Danger Zone"! I was about to be on *World's Wildest Police Videos*! The driver pulled over quickly and disappointment began to set in. I had been hoping for some high-speed, low-drag awesomeness. I was about to settle for just one ticket.

No, wait! The driver bailed out of the car and made a beeline for the woods! This guy apparently had no clue where he was stopped. There was nothing but miles of swamp land on either side of the highway, and he just ran full speed into the thick of it.

Foot chase! I was jumping over fallen trees, avoiding the big puddles and tree branches. My P.F. Flyers helped me run faster and jump higher. Every time I got a little closer, he got a little farther away. He must have had a pair too. A worthy opponent! The weeds were getting thicker and thicker the farther in I ventured. The spider webs were getting bigger. The air in my lungs was emptying and I had lost sight of him, but I could still hear him in the distance. About a half mile into the wetlands, the darkness was really setting in. The sun slowly faded away and darkness started to fill the swamp. I pulled out my handy dandy flashlight and slowed my pace. Soon it was as dark as…well…night.

Well, Momma didn't raise a quitter, so I kept on trekking into the abyss. I refused to be the guy who let the out-of-towner outrun me. No sir! I was ducking and dodging the vines, hopping over the dead trees and splashing through the water trying to catch up to him. My hope started to dwindle and reality set in. Wouldn't you know it? Right about the time I was thinking to myself, *"He's gone. I'll just go back to my car,"* it happened. The flashlight slowly started to dwindle down to nothing. Nothing except a small little glowing ember that reminded me of how dumb I was for not having fresh batteries. The glow faded to nothing. Perfect. Now I was in the middle of the South Georgia swamp. At night. In the dark. Alone. And with no flashlight. Just perfect.

It was quite an eerie feeling being alone in the middle of a swamp surrounded by darkness and not knowing which way is out. I was so far into the swamp that I couldn't hear the cars on the interstate. I walked slowly with my hands out in front of me hoping they found whatever was in front of me before my face found it. Lower hanging branches managed to avoid my hands and poke my head. I walked into those monster spider webs then did the "it's crawling on me" death dance!

While dancing through the swamp, I tripped on something and landed in the mud. Did I land feet away from a snake? An alligator? The guy I was chasing through the swamp in the first place? I didn't know because I couldn't see! It. Was. Pitch. Black! Doom and gloom may have had me surrounded, and I wouldn't have had a single clue. There was nothing more I wanted in that moment than to see someone with a flashlight.

Not having anything better to do than ponder my recent life choices, I asked myself, *"How did I even get in this predicament?"* I saw that man run into a swamp that I knew I had no business going in. Some of y'all know how pride can be when it really grabs ahold of you. It got me. I just had to chase him. Now I was waiting and hoping to find my way back to safety. Slowly and cautiously, I took baby steps through the swamp looking and listening for anything that would bring me closer to safety.

Have you ever been in a dark spot in your life after chasing something you know you had no business chasing? It starts off with just a friendly conversation with the lady at the office and the next thing you know, you're in an affair with someone who isn't your wife. *"How did I get in this predicament?"* A friend offers you an anti-anxiety pill to help you relax and a few weeks later, you're popping pills like they're Skittles. *"How did I get in this spot?"* You're strolling through your social media when you come across a friend in some rather revealing clothing. The mind starts to wander and the next thing you know, you're hooked on the porn industry. *"How did*

I get here?" One drink to take the edge off has you stopping by the liquor store every night on the way home. *"How did I end up here?"*

I read a story about a man who found himself in a dark place. He started out great—he had plenty of family around him, a nice house, and plenty of food. I imagine he had some the latest clothing, a comfortable bed, and anything that he could really desire at his fingertips. But for some reason beyond my comprehension, it wasn't enough. He wanted to pursue a life he had no business pursuing. He desired the far country. You know him as the prodigal. Luke 15:11-24 reads:

> *A certain man had two sons. And the younger of them said to his father, "Father, give me the portion of goods that falls to me." So he divided to them his livelihood. And not many days after, the younger son gathered all together, journeyed to a far country, and there wasted his possessions with prodigal living. But when he had spent all, there arose a severe famine in that land, and he began to be in want. Then he went and joined himself to a citizen of that country, and he sent him into his fields to feed swine. And he would gladly have filled his stomach with the pods that the swine ate, and no one gave him anything.*
>
> *But when he came to himself, he said, "How many of my father's hired servants have bread enough and to spare, and I perish with hunger! I will arise and go to my father, and will say to him, 'Father, I have sinned against heaven and before you, and I am no longer worthy to be called your son. Make me like one of your hired servants.'"*
>
> *And he arose and came to his father. But when he was still a great way off, his father saw him and had compassion, and ran and fell on his neck and kissed him. And the son said*

to him, "Father, I have sinned against heaven and in your sight, and am no longer worthy to be called your son."

But the father said to his servants, "Bring out the best robe and put it on him, and put a ring on his hand and sandals on his feet. And bring the fatted calf here and kill it, and let us eat and be merry; for this my son was dead and is alive again; he was lost and is found." And they began to be merry.

I've had the opportunity to talk to many people who have fallen into these types of situations. My patrol shift was dispatched to a single vehicle accident during a bad storm. Our dispatchers reported that the truck was in a deep ditch and filling with water, and the driver was unable to get out. We found a large pickup truck with its nose just buried in water. The cab was filled with water and the driver was having a really difficult time trying to get out of the truck. Being hammered drunk probably didn't help his cause.

I knew the man's family, but I had never met him personally. It was such a sad situation. He was a very good businessman, had a lovely wife, two very well-behaved kids, nice cars, a huge house, and a six-figure salary. But he developed a love for alcohol, so much so that his body needed alcohol to function. He had to stay in some type of drunken stupor. If he didn't have alcohol running through his veins, he would get very sick going through withdrawal. Everything he did required a drink. If he was going to go to one of his kids' baseball games, he'd have to stop by the liquor store on the way. One the way home from work, he'd stop and get himself a sip. Mowing the grass required a few beers. He was consumed by it.

Living that kind of life, it doesn't take too long for everything to start falling apart. The DUI (Driving Under the Influence) charges he racked up cost him his license. He couldn't get to work so he lost his job. The family couldn't afford the house, so the bank foreclosed on it. His wife left him and took the kids with her. His family didn't want anything to do with him anyway. He was truly starving in the pig pen, desiring to be fed the scraps. Unfortunately, I don't know that he has come to his senses about the empty promises of the far country. Pray for that man. Pray for his family.[1]

Patrolling in my own little Mayberry, I come across more than my fair share of homeless people. Some are homeless by choice, some by choices not of their own. Others find themselves in their situation because they believed the lies they heard about the far country. A younger man I know came from a middle-class family, didn't heed his parents' advice on how to be a decent human, and now he wanders up and down the highway looking for spare change or half-smoked cigarettes. Any money he can find goes to buying methamphetamine or alcohol. It's sad. He too hasn't seen the light. Pray for that man, too.

The far country is a place filled with broken promises and shattered dreams. It lures people with the hope of a good time. Many will travel there to be carefree—to eat, drink and be merry. They want to be their own boss and live without rules. When I picture the "far country" in my mind, I picture a Las Vegas-style city. There are bright flashy lights, huge buildings, people laughing, and expensive cars in an oasis in the desert. The far country screams, "Come here and all your dreams will come true." But, when your dreams aren't aligned with Biblical principles, you end up in the pig pen wallowing in the aftermath of your carefree living.

It took just a few short verses for this young man to go from Cloud 9 to rock bottom to then walking the humble road home. You and I only spend a few seconds reading over them. I imagine

---

1. After writing this chapter, I learned from his wife that he passed away from alcohol poisoning.

that for his father though, those were the longest verses of the father's life. The son's road back to his home couldn't have been an easy journey. The man had nothing left—no money, no food, and nowhere to stay. He had a long journey home. This wasn't some trip back from the next-door neighbor's; this was a journey. A long, hard, painful journey.

My adventure getting out of that swamp was nowhere near as difficult as the prodigal's journey home. After gathering my bearings, I slowly started moving back to where I thought civilization was. I took small, cautious steps. I was already lost—I didn't need to be stepping in a snake hole or into a gator nest. I could hear the cars driving down the highway, but I couldn't see them. As I inched closer and closer, I saw the flashlights from other officers punching through the trees showing me the way out. It was the light from other officers that brought me out of the darkness. Lesson learned: Never chase someone somewhere you know you shouldn't be chasing anyone. And carry a backup flashlight.

How did the prodigal son do it? The same way you overcome whatever is standing between you and God. You take it one step at a time, and you never quit. I don't know where you might be on the prodigal road. You might be back home with the Father, and that's great! Keep up the hard work. Keep that faith strong. You might be struggling with an addiction of some sort or doubting your faith. Maybe someone other than your spouse has caught your eye and you're getting pulled towards adultery. Whatever it is, God is waiting for you. He is crazy about you. He loves you to a degree that our little human minds have a hard time comprehending.

Can you imagine the relief that the prodigal felt as he came over that last hill or around that last curve? He came into view of his father who rushed out to meet him! I picture this son having torn clothing, worn-out sandals (if any shoes at all), starving, and his throat nearly dry from dehydration. As soon as he found out that his father was going to accept him back as his son, even though he knew he wasn't worthy—oh the flood of emotions that must have overtaken him. What a relief! What an indescribable feeling! He had traveled so far and overcome so much, and he had finally made it back. He wouldn't have to worry about being hungry or thirsty or where he would sleep. He was home.

Was the far country worth it? Of course not. As soon as the money ran out, the hard times came. But was that long journey home worth it? Absolutely! His travel home was probably some of the hardest times he had ever encountered. But he made it—one step at a time. Now he was home with his family, but he was also a strong warning for any of his friends who want to make the journey to the far country. Imagine what he would have to say to those who want to travel by that road! What a powerful story he had to tell them! A story about how he was so well taken care of but threw it all away, and yet God was still ever present.

If you find yourself on that road to the far country, please make the u-turn. The juice isn't worth the squeeze. Maybe you're on your way home—don't give up. The road is full of challenges, hills and valleys—don't quit! You keep going. There are plenty of people who will try and pull you back, probably more than those who would help push you forward—pay them no mind. If they aren't encouraging you to come home to your Father, ignore them. You're not on the prodigal road anymore. You're on Heaven's road.

WORDS TO WEIGH

1. What are some of the lures of the "far country" for various age groups today? What things might Christians believe the world can give them that cannot be found in the Christian life?

2. How should we handle these temptations? List a few verses to help you when temptations arise and memorize them. How can you apply these verses to real-life situations that you may face?

3. Pride was touched on briefly in this chapter. What does the Bible say about pride? List a few verses.

4. In what ways can pride lead us to the "far country"? Is this only for those who are full of themselves? Can pride affect our actions if we believe we'll never be the ones to fall?

5. Look at your answers to these questions and think about the temptations you face. Now, look at the Bible verses and your real-life applications. Make a plan for when these times arise.

CH. 3
The Lambo

I was driving around my little city doing cop things in the fall of 2014—a pretty calm (we don't say *quiet*) afternoon. The tones dropped and our dispatcher reported a possible car on fire at the pumps at a gas station. This wasn't a call I would usually go to because, at the time, I was a traffic cop. However, being the police makes you nosy and curious so I decided I'd go check it out. Maybe I'd get some cool dash cam footage of the gas station exploding. Maybe they'd use it on the national news. Either way, this call had some potential of being a good war story later.

It was kind of a letdown when I pulled up and saw the fire was out. It was nearly a waste of time—I almost just drove away, but first I decided to check out the damage. The car was gone. There wasn't anything left of it, save the rims and a piece of the rear bumper. Those rims—I'd seen those rims before. I knew this wasn't your typical Mustang GT, Corvette, or Porsche. I whipped into the parking lot and then my suspicions became reality. I almost had a breakdown. I felt like a teenage girl who just found out all the tickets to the Justin Bieber concert were sold out. My heart dropped all the way to the ground. The car, a dream car of mine, was a pile of ashes and scrap. It was a yellow Lamborghini Gallardo.

I met the driver of the car. He was a nice man in his early 60s fresh into retirement, casually dressed in Levi's jeans and a button up flannel shirt. And he wasn't crying. I was more upset than he was that his car—that costs more than my house—was now a stain on the concrete of a local gas station. Maybe the man was just in shock? Maybe it hadn't hit him yet that his super car wasn't going home with him? Or maybe he was just crazy? I asked him if he was going to be okay and his reply confirmed my suspicions. "It is okay. It is just a car." Yup, that man was crazy. Just over 1,000 of these cars were ever made. His just got roasted and all he has to say is, "It is just a car"! It's not like his insurance can just go find him another one! "It is just a car." If Thor didn't ride lightning, he would have used this car! "It is just a car." This man had completely lost his mind!

The car was a retirement gift he and his wife bought for themselves just after retiring. They weren't poor by any means, but they also weren't super rich either. The man enjoyed the car, but in the grand scheme of his life, it was just a car. He was okay and his wife was okay. The car was just that—a car.

Photo: The picture I took at the scene.

Jesus tells us to "lay up for yourselves treasures in Heaven, where neither moth nor rust destroys and where thieves do not break in and steal. For where your treasure is, there your heart will be also" (Matthew 6:20-21). That's a fancy way of suggesting not to get stuck in your stuff because it is just stuff. The real treasure isn't on earth. It's in Heaven.

I went to a fight call between teenagers at our high school some time ago. One teen was walking through a crowded hallway, and, in the hustle and bustle, he accidentally stepped on the other teen's brand-new Nike shoes. A small smudge equated to justification to throw haymakers. This teen was livid that someone had the audacity to step on his new Nikes, even accidentally. You'd have thought someone had shot his mother. He was seriously stuck in his stuff.

In the real world outside of the high school hallways, no one really cares what you have on your feet. What is more important is what is in your heart. Treating people like they were actually made in the image and likeness of God (Genesis 1:27). What if that teen, instead of going MMA on the other teen, had found compassion and forgiveness for the other teen's mistake? What kind of impact would that have had? What kind of difference could he have made in the other young man's life? What if you and I put more value in people than we did our stuff?

I've been to accident scenes that were very minor. Like, you couldn't tell where one car hit the other. Yet, the driver who got hit loses his mind that his car got bumped by Grandma backing out of a parking space. The ironic part is when the driver cussing Grandma has a Jesus fish decal on his bumper or a "Follow me to church" sticker. "These people…honor Me with their lips [or car decals in this case!], but their heart is far from Me" (Matthew 15:8).

Jesus challenged a rich ruler to sell everything he had and give it to the poor (Luke 18:19). The man was so discouraged because he was incredibly wealthy and had a lot of stuff. But wait, wasn't he a great person? Didn't he keep all the commandments? Didn't he have the Jesus fish decal on the back of his wagons? Sure, but Jesus knew the problem this young man had—his heart wasn't focused where it should be. Now I'm not saying it's wrong to have nice things, but I want to challenge you to keep your focus on Jesus and His Kingdom.

You might find yourself in a place like where I was not too long ago. I was chasing that overtime—chasing that dollar. I cared more about making money than spending time with my family. Any opportunity I could get to work, I did. My department offered extra duty details in December called Jingle Bell Patrol. We could come in on our off days and work an extra six hours in the evening. I worked 29 days that December—all while missing out on worship services, bedtimes with my kids, dinners with my wife. And for what? A few extra dollars. My heart was far from God.

The things you and I possess are just that—things. The people we could impact for Jesus aren't just people—they're souls that Jesus died to save. Jesus dying for them makes them more valuable than all the Lamborghinis ever made.

WORDS TO WEIGH

1. Name a time you found yourself putting too much value on your "Lambos." How did it affect your walk with God?

2. How does the devil and the world use the focus on acquiring things to harm us spiritually? What will happen to our souls if we only focus on things and neglect our souls? Find a verse that states this.

3. How might others around us act differently when we value people like Jesus did in the New Testament? List some verses with examples of people He said had value.

4. What steps can you take to ensure your focus doesn't become possession-centered instead of Christ-centered? Find a few verses that will help you.

CH. 4
Remember What Judas Forgot

> *Then Judas, His betrayer, seeing that He had been condemned, was remorseful and brought back the thirty pieces of silver to the chief priests and elders, saying, "I have sinned by betraying innocent blood." And they said, "What is that to us? You see to it!" Then he threw down the pieces of silver in the temple and departed, and went and hanged himself (Matthew 27:3-5).*

I can't wrap my mind around what was going through Judas' head during these last moments. He had literally walked side by side with Jesus. He had talked with Jesus. He had watched Him restore sight, heal the wounded, and raise the dead. He heard His message of redemption straight from the Savior's own mouth! He was there for all of it! Yet he still sold Him for a little bit of silver. Then overtaken by grief, he took his own life. Judas forgot something very important about his life.

Having responded to a plethora of suicide calls over the years and having spoken with many families who have lost someone to suicide, one contributing factor seems to resonate with their stories: a feeling of worthlessness. I usually hear that the victim was battling depression, the loss of a job, a debilitating illness, PTSD, divorce, etc., and from those battles came a feeling of worthlessness. When I say *worthless*, I don't mean it in a sense that no one likes you. I mean a sense of worthlessness where you feel you shouldn't be on this earth anymore and when you're gone, no one will notice. This worthless isn't something you can just "get over." It's more like a long journey over a high mountain covered in ice. You must tread carefully. One wrong step or word spoken, and you're sliding all the way back to where you started: worthless. To climb this mountain, you must have the right shoes, the right gloves, the right gear, and, more importantly, the right mindset.

On January 11, 2012, I responded to a house where a 10-year-old girl had committed suicide. She was watching TV with her siblings and wanted to play a game. Her siblings denied her request, so she went to her room alone. There she placed a belt around her neck and ended her life. She left a small note explaining that she was sorry for being a burden to her family and hoped they would be better off without her.

A few summers ago, I delivered a death notification to a Marine after his 15-year-old son ended his life by a self-inflicted gunshot. I've gone into a house where a dad turned his car on in the garage and slowly went to sleep in the driver's seat, ending his life. He thought his baby girl would be better off without her daddy because of mistakes he made. I've gone to a home where an elderly lady ended her life during a drunken stupor after having a petty argument with her boyfriend. All these precious souls either didn't know or forgot how much meaning their lives possessed.

When was the last time you read John 3:16? We all know it. But when was the last time you really read it and then really pondered what it is that verse is saying? I sum up John 3:16 like this: You're valuable. Incredibly valuable. You have a value that you really can't comprehend. Our finite brains really can't understand the depths of an infinite notion that "God so loved" you and me. The One who created the stars, the oceans, the mountains, the grass, and winds also created you. He knows your name. He knows how many hairs are on your head. If He knows those fine details of your life, He also knows the struggle going on in your heart—the heart that He created.

If I asked you who was Jacob's wife, could you tell me? Did you say Rachel? Would you happen to remember his other wife's name? Don't feel bad if you forgot—plenty of people have. She's an easy character to pass over. Here's a quick refresher for you guys who forgot.

In Genesis 29, Jacob had struck a deal with Laban that he would work seven years in exchange for Rachel's hand in marriage (vs. 18). Seven years pass, and Jacob came to collect on the deal. The wedding ceremony was performed, and the following morning Jacob woke up to realize that woman lying next to him was not Rachel as he intended, but rather her older sister—Leah! #awkward. Jacob then had to work another seven years to receive Rachel as his bride.

If anyone has ever had a reason to feel worthless, Leah had plenty. Her father literally had to trick someone into marrying her. Throughout their marriage, Jacob loved Rachel more than her (vs. 30). Can you imagine being married to someone who doesn't love you, didn't want to marry you in the first place, and every time they look at you, they wish you were your sibling? It really can't get much worse. Scripture also describes Leah as being "hated" (vs. 31). She thought if she had his children, he would love her, but that plan failed. Despite all that Leah went through, she was extremely valuable in God's eyes. Let me prove it.

You may recall that Jacob had a couple sons—12 to be exact. Most people, when they think of Jacob and his sons, follow the more popular wife Rachel and her son Joseph. The same Joseph who went on to help save the people in Egypt. However, Leah had several sons too. One went by the name Judah. Why is Judah important you ask? If you skim through those genealogies in Matthew 1 and Luke 3, you'll find that through Judah came the "only begotten Son" (John 3:16). One cannot tell the entire story of God's love for the world without Leah. That wife that you and I casually skim over in the Scriptures is in the same lineage as Jesus. Let that sink in for a few seconds. Leah, having gone through all she went through, was incredibly valuable to God's plan for our salvation. Without Leah, we don't get Jesus.

Leah is a strong reminder to us of how much worth we have in God's eyes. If someone in Leah's position can be that valuable to God in the plan to bring Jesus into this world, how much more valuable are you—someone that Son died to save? It is written that "there is joy in the presence of the angels of God over one sinner that repents" (Luke 15:10). When you and I change our minds to do God's will— the angels are rejoicing! You are so valuable to God that He allowed His Son to leave a place that has no pain, fear, or hurt so that He could be beaten, abandoned, betrayed, alone, hungry, and ultimately killed so you and I can go home to Heaven. I want to encourage you and let you know that no matter what you are going through, suicide isn't the answer. You are too valuable in the eyes of God.

You might be in that relationship that is falling apart, struggling with drugs/alcohol or coping with the death of a loved one. Maybe you are just feeling alone or have done some things in the past you deeply regret. None of that changes your value to God. None of it. Nothing can "separate us from the love of God" (Romans 8:39). God places that much value on you—not the tress, animals, or oceans—but on you! He wants you to live! He wants you to live and tell everyone else who has lost their way how valuable they are to Him. Your life has value no matter where you are in life! Remember what Judas forgot.

WORDS TO WEIGH

1. Let's piggyback off our last question from the previous chapter: Jesus continually showed that people of all different backgrounds, cultures, experiences, and pasts had value. Take note of who they are and what they had done. Most importantly, look at the value they had to the kingdom. How did Jesus view them?

2. What ways did these people contribute to spreading the Gospel? How can God use ALL of you (your past, experiences, trauma, culture, etc.) to further the Gospel today?

3. Because God is the same yesterday, today, and tomorrow, He sees your value as much as He did theirs. Look up some verses that tell you who/what God says you are. Pick at least two verses to write down and remember when you question your worth. Post them in a prominent place as a reminder.

4. What insecurities do you face? Do you know there are verses to counteract every one of them? With the help of good ol' Google, research what the Bible says about an insecurity or weakness you struggle with. God's Word has a remedy for all.

CH. 5
I've Got a Mansion

My shift responded to a call at a very well-to-do neighborhood. I say *neighborhood*, but it could have been its own little city. This neighborhood was a gated community with private security—no getting past the front gate without a personal invitation from a member. You couldn't just go in and drive around. They had their own golf course—a nice golf course too. You could have eaten off the greens. It had a private restaurant that sat right on the river. The members had their own spa and massage parlor. There were several horse barns and horse trails. Each member spent tens of thousands of dollars in fees to live here. It was fancy.

The mansion we went to was equally as fancy. This mansion was nestled next to a small pond and surrounded by Georgia oak trees draped in Spanish moss. The driveway led to a three-car garage with some very luxurious cars and SUVs. The lawn was meticulously managed. The bushes were cut to perfection. In the back there was a custom pool with a slide, a waterfall feature, and a diving board. It had a covered screened back porch with very comfy-looking outdoor furniture. It was fancy.

We walked inside and it looked like the place jumped right out of a magazine. There wasn't a speck of dust anywhere. Large pieces of artwork were all over the walls. The kitchen had some serious hardware—top of the line appliances. The fridge was hidden in the cabinets. There was a double-stack oven, two sinks, and the biggest fridge I've ever seen. It even had a TV built into the door. Why you need a TV in your fridge, I don't know. But they had it. The study room had custom built wall-to-wall, floor-to-ceiling shelving with hidden compartments. Whoever these people were, they were living a good life.

Or so I thought.

We were there for a report of a deceased person. The husband had come home and found his wife dead, lying on her side in the bed. Her nightstand had a large bottle of vodka sitting next to several bottles of strong pain pills. We opened the drawer to her nightstand and found several more bottles of vodka. I glanced into the bathroom—more bottles of vodka, some full and some empty. It looked like half the liquor store had been purchased. No foul play was suspected; it seemed obvious what had taken place. Come to find out, the two had been going through a rough marriage for several years. The wife tried to drown her sorrows with the alcohol and numb the pain with the pills. She went to sleep but never woke up. This house reminds me of a couple things.

One, this family reminds me of how we portray ourselves on social media. Very rarely will you see people post pictures about what their lives are really like outside of social media. You never see someone post pictures of them arguing with their spouse or children. We don't post pictures of the bills that aren't paid. We don't post about job loss, depression, addiction, the children who don't listen, or any other negative circumstance in life. We always post pictures of us smiling together, our hair looks good, the children pretending like they like each other, the cars are clean, and our perfect house is in the background. Everything looks perfect. And that's all we show the world.

We don't want people to know that we are, in fact, struggling. We don't want people to know that we are broken, hurting, and very close to killing each other. If people knew that we have real problems, they'd think we are failures. They'll judge us. They'll look down on us. We'll be embarrassed that our lives aren't like a Hallmark movie.

It's even more crazy that we pretend like this in the church too! We come to the worship assembly and, just before we pull into the parking lot, we give everyone the pep talk. "Don't you say another word about *x*, *y*, *z* in here, or you'll get it when we get home. Now everyone, get out the car, put your best smile on, and get to Bible class." Then we all walk into the building pretending life is just as we post on our social media—perfect. We try to be like Moses covering his face so the people wouldn't see his shining skin begin to fade (2 Corinthians 3:13). We don't want everyone knowing that our perfect family/life/whatever isn't so perfect, so we put that mask on and pretend everything is okay.

Maybe it's time we as a church take off that mask. When was the last time you asked a fellow Christian to pray for you? You don't have to air out your dirty laundry to them, but a simple "Can you pray for me?" can have an enormous impact. They'll know you trust them to pray for them. They'll have the opportunity to approach the throne room of God Himself with a petition on your behalf. What if we as the church take off those masks and stop pretending? What if we actually "confess our faults one to another, and pray for one another…" (James 5:16, KJV) and be the church that Jesus died to save?

Second, walking up to that house, I was envious. You could fit my house in their garage. It's easy to see what someone else has and wish you had just a piece of it. From the outside looking in, they were living the dream. People who have that nice of an estate don't have those kinds of problems. If I could just get that nice house, fill my garage with those cars, cook my food in those ovens, relax in that pool, and read a book in that study—life would be perfect. How do you have problems when you have everything money can buy? That's the dream, right? To have the nicest stuff?

One of the hardest parts, in at least my life, has been finding contentment. That's been my battle. I've never struggled with alcohol or drug addiction. They offer me no temptation. You could have a kilogram of the purest Columbian bam-bam (cocaine) in front of me—I wouldn't think twice about partaking. You could give me a bottle of the finest Tennessee sipping whiskey and I would have no problem dumping it down the sink. But being content with the physical things I have—there is my struggle. It's taken me years and years to get to a point where I feel like I'm in, at least in some sense, content with my physical possessions.

Sometimes I think about how nice it would be having such that mansion on that large plot of land with a garage full of the finest rides (maybe a nice yellow Lamborghini). While I know I probably will never be able to afford any of those—cops are not really known for their large bank accounts—would I buy them if I could? Would I try to obtain them if I knew the real cost? What would I have to sacrifice to get them? Would having that large mansion, large bank account, nice cars, flashy jewelry, etc., be worth it if it cost me my marriage? If it cost me missing out on all those memories with my kids? If it costs me hearing, "Well done, good and faithful servant" (Matthew 25:23)? A lot of times we see things others have and wish we had that life, but we don't really stop and consider what it would cost us, apart from money, to have them.

A man at my home congregation told us of a time where he had an opportunity to invest into a local bank. This investment was a gold mine for sure. He declined the offer to invest because he knew it would be too much money for him. He knew that amount of money would take him away from God and he wasn't willing do it. "For what will it profit a man if he gains the whole world, and loses his own soul?" (Mark 8:36).

Paul told the Philippian brethren, "Not that I speak in regard to need, for I have learned in whatever state I am, to be content" (Philippians 4:11). Paul had to learn contentment, just like I am learning. I saw a

Facebook meme once that showed someone riding a bike watching someone drive by in a car. "I wish I had a car." Then there was a picture of someone walking who was watching the guy on the bike. "I wish I had a bike." Then there was a picture of a kid in a wheelchair watching the guy walking. "I wish I could walk." Someone right now is wishing they had the blessing you may not be thankful for.

Perhaps instead of looking at what others have and wishing you had their stuff, let's learn to be content with the blessings God has already provided us. Let's be satisfied with "just a cottage below, a littler silver and a little gold" because as followers of Christ we have a "mansion just over the hilltop in that land where we'll never grow old."[2]

WORDS TO WEIGH

1. Name times when you or people you know have not been content. What impact did that have on your/their Christian walk?

2. What is the difference between striving to make a better life for yourself versus not being content? How would you define *contentment*? How does the Bible define contentment?

3. If we are grateful for what we've been given instead of longing for what we don't have, what impact would that have in our battle for contentment? List some verses on gratitude that can help us.

4. What are a few ways to guard our hearts and minds as we attain material things in this life?

---

2. Stanphill, Ira. Lyrics to "Mansion Over the Hilltop." Genius, https://genius.com/Ira-stanphill-mansion-over-the-hilltop-lyrics.

CH. 6
Feed My Sheep

Having worked on a patrol shift for nearly a decade, I began looking for a new adventure in my career. As my luck would have it, a new opportunity presented itself. Our high school of around 2,000 students needed a new School Resource Officer (SRO). Who would give up their fast car and bad-guy chasing 14 days a month schedule to go work in a cinderblock jungle filled with hormonal crazed teenagers five days a week? Teenagers who didn't know how to use deodorant, didn't wear enough clothes, thought every inconvenience was a mid-life crisis, and referred to you as "bruh"? I would…

The schedule worked out well for me, surprisingly enough. I quickly slipped into a routine, and it became almost second nature for me. Instead of having to deal with the chaos and uncertainty of a patrol shift, my day was set in stone. I arrived at 7:30 in the morning for traffic duty. It was like a real-life game of *Frogger*. I dodged either the little speed demons as they whipped into the school parking lot in a race against the bell or the parents who were late for work and giving their little angel a lesson on how to "tuck and roll."

Then I made a few rounds through the hallways and then it was off to the gym. The coach let me keep some peanut butter and jelly in his office so I could have a morning snack. Ain't nothing better than a good ol' pb & j. "Straight slaps" as the kids say (that means it tastes good. I didn't know either—don't feel bad). I had to be quick in my sandwich making. High schoolers have the hearing capabilities of a brick, but they can smell food like a shark smells blood, just better. As soon as the seal was broken on the peanut butter, here they came. I'd have to shut the door, pretend I wasn't there, and just hope they'd go away. Okay, it wasn't that bad…most days.

I remember sitting in the office when this young freshman came in while I was in the middle of stuffing my face.

"Hey Officer Z, can I get a sandwich?"

"You sure can't."

"Please, I didn't get breakfast."

"Sounds to me like you need to wake up earlier and get some then."

"My mom doesn't give me breakfast."

"Tell her I said to give you breakfast."

"Please?"

"No…"

We had a similar conversation for about a week before he finally stopped coming and asking me. Ah, peace at last. There really isn't anything more peaceful than a nice quiet snack.

About two weeks later I was called to one of the assistant principal's office where I saw this kid sitting in front of his desk. He had been crying and looked defeated. The principal pulled me to the side to explain what he had just been told. The freshman came to his office to say that his family only fed him one meal a day and didn't provide him with the basic necessities.

I went to ask him about his home life, and he told me the same thing. He only got one meal (if you could even call it a meal) per day. I asked him why he didn't come tell me sooner, and his response knocked the wind out of me. "I tried. You didn't listen." I called the shift supervisor and one of my detectives. Come to find out, when he got home, he was locked in a shed attached to the carport at his house. He had an old mattress to sleep on, and a small metal bucket was his toilet. His parents (if you could even call them such) were starving him.

"Depart from Me…for I was hungry and you gave Me no food" (Matthew 25:41-42). That verse haunts me to this day. I had an opportunity to show the love of God to this young impressionable soul and failed. I had the opportunity to be the light in the young man's life, but I wasn't. I could have been the difference he needed me to be. Every time I read this passage or hear it, I go back to that office where I enjoyed a sandwich in peace while he was starving. I suppose I could tell you that I didn't give him a sandwich because I didn't want to be the cause of him getting sick. Or that I didn't know if he had any allergies. Or it was against our policy to give him food that wasn't approved by the school board. But those would all be lies. I just didn't want to be bothered to make him a sandwich. Plain and simple. He was a burden I didn't want to bear.

The Department of Family and Children Services came and removed him from the home, and his parents were arrested. I never saw or heard from the kid again. But that event caused a great change in my life. Never again would I see someone hungry and not give him food. Never again would I be the Levite or the priest and pass by someone in need (Luke 10:31-32). Jesus told Peter, "Feed My sheep" (John 21:17), and I decided to take that literally.

Over the next five years of working at the school, I made it my mission to always have some sort of food item with me, or at least accessible to me. I would walk down the halls with a box of Chips Deluxe cookies (they also "straight slap"), and if you passed by me I'd offer you one.

Nothing makes the day better than a Chips Deluxe cookie. I became known for randomly dropping into classes with food for everyone. One Friday night before a big rival football game, I went to our two grocery stores and bought all the Sour Patch candy I could find. Then at the start of the second quarter, I threw it all into the student section. It was pretty wild seeing how crazy they got over some Sour Patch.

I wasn't trying to get them to like me, per se; I was getting them to trust me. Getting a high schooler to trust a cop, especially in this era, was difficult and took time. But my plan to get to their hearts went right through their stomachs. I think Jesus subtly taught that in the Scriptures. When we read the Gospel accounts of all the miracles Jesus did while on earth, we see He raised a few dead people, He brought sight to some blind people, and He healed some illnesses and some injuries. But how many people did He feed? Thousands.

In Matthew 14, Jesus had just learned that John the Baptist had been beheaded. He went to a deserted place, and this massive crowd followed Him. Jesus, having compassion on them, healed their sick and as the hour grew late, his disciples suggested that he send them away so they could essentially fend for themselves in getting some food. "But Jesus said to them, 'They do not need to go away. YOU give them something to eat'" (vs. 16, emp. mine). I feel like I would have been one of Jesus' disciples in this story. I picture me and Jesus hanging out in the coach's office and here comes this little freshman bugging us for food. "Jesus, send this little freshman away so he can go home and get his own food." All they had to feed these 5,000 people was a few fish and a couple loaves of bread. All I had to feed that freshman was a can of peanut butter and some bread. Jesus fed the 5,000; I sent one away hungry. I'm a firm believer and am whole-heartedly convinced that if you want to show people God's love, you feed them.

I was at Polishing the Pulpit some years ago and got to have dinner with one of my heroes and his family. He bought mine. Not because

I didn't have money (I mean, I am a cop, so I didn't have a ton), but because he wanted to show God's love to me. He told me he cared about me without saying a word. I don't remember a single meal I had that week, except that one. People will always remember that time they were hungry and you fed them. Even if it's just a "slapping" pb and j.

You want to make an impact on that new couple visiting your congregation? Feed them. Want to show your coworkers God's love? Feed them. Have a family you know that is struggling to make ends meet? Cook dinner for them. Have a widow or widower in your congregation? Invite them over for lunch one day. Share a meal and spend time with them. Invest a little food in your ministry. It'll pay dividends, both here and in eternity. Feed His sheep.

▮━▮ WORDS TO WEIGH

1. Name some people in your local congregation who seem lonely or need some encouragement. Invite one of them to a meal this week, even if it's coffee and donuts (cop food!).

2. Think of a time when you had a meaningful meal or time with someone. What made it special? Look for ways this week to reach out to someone. Whether it's food, a card, or a text—let someone know that you're thinking about them.

3. Meet with your friends or your youth group. Together, make a plan to feed and reach out to people who are hurting or struggling in your circle or congregation. Look for those on the "fringe" who need fed either physically or spiritually.

4. How can you use feeding people to bring them to Christ? Consider neighbors, widows, those grieving, homeless, or sick.

CH. 7
When Sheep Turn into Wolves

"Local Officer Charged with Child Molestation" was how the headline read. There was so much wrong with that headline, I didn't know where to start. Especially since this guy worked with me. The outcry was great and swift. Every news agency around was at our doorstep wanting to interview anyone who worked with him, anyone he had arrested, or anyone who followed him on Facebook. We couldn't go anywhere without someone hounding us wanting some of the "tea." (*Tea* is Southern talk for gossip).

Trust in a small town is difficult to re-build when it's broken. Honestly, who is going to trust you once someone who dressed like you do every day is charged with one of the most heinous crimes ever written down? It was less than fun going to work for the next few weeks. I often wondered how many people didn't come to us for help because of what he did. How many victims of sexual assaults didn't want to come speak with us because of him? How many lives could have been changed for the better if he wouldn't have done what he did? He was sentenced to 10 years in federal prison.

Just Google "Officer charged with…" and let Google fill in the blank. It's sickening what pops up. Officer charged with assault, DUI, murder, theft, etc. The list goes on and on. Trust between the police departments and the community is destroyed. Even if the incident took place somewhere across the country, the ripples can be seen everywhere. When the police violate their oath of office, it impacts more than just them—it impacts the entire department.

I know of an officer who was called to the interstate for a pedestrian walking in the roadway. The man was clearly in a state of mental distress and had no business being on the busy interstate. Yet, the officer, not wanting to be bothered with the headache of having to sit with this man at the hospital for a few hours while an evaluation is completed, leaves him on the interstate. "We ain't got time to be dealing with this." A few hours later and a few miles north of where he was first seen, the man was struck by a semi-truck and killed.

That same scenario has played out in congregations all over the world. People in desperate need of the love found only in Jesus are shown the door. My wife and I have a saying we constantly impress on our boys. "You have no idea what someone else is going through." We always try to remind them to be kind, because they could be the difference between someone staying in the church or walking away. They could be the one that says something that saves his or her life. So can you if you choose to be compassionate. You have no idea what someone sitting right beside you is going through.

I went to help a sheriff's deputy with a domestic dispute outside of my city. I pulled up to the house, and as soon as I walked in, my spirit plummeted. It was a husband and wife that we sat beside at church for the last several years. He was explaining that he had been having an affair and was leaving his wife to go be with the other woman. The wife was distraught, he was in a panic, and I was completely lost in the situation. We had been right beside them every Sunday singing songs, praying, and worshipping. Every Sunday! The church was looking at him to be a future leader in the church. His wife taught ladies' classes. They were the best of the best—and we had no clue what they were really going through. And we have no idea what anyone else in the congregation is really going through or what they may have gone through in the past.

The lady sitting by herself could be going home to an abusive husband. A husband in your Bible class could be fighting alcoholism or an addiction to pills. That young man could be thinking today is the day he ends his life. The young lady could be a whisper away from walking away from the church because of how she had been treated when she needed the church the most. You never know. And you never know what impact your kindness and encouragement might have on them.

Check out this example from Exodus 17. This is so good:

> *Now Amalek came and fought with Israel in Rephidim. And Moses said to Joshua, "Choose us some men and go out, fight with Amalek. Tomorrow I will stand on the top of the hill with the rod of God in my hand." So, Joshua did as Moses said to him and fought with Amalek. And Moses, Aaron, and Hur went up to the top of the hill. And so it was, when Moses held up his hand, that Israel prevailed; and when he let down his hand, Amalek prevailed. But Moses' hands became heavy; so they took a stone and put it under him, and he sat on it. And Aaron and Hur supported his hands, one on one side, and the other on the other side; and his hands were steady until the going down of the sun. So Joshua defeated Amalek and his people with the edge of the sword (vs. 8-13).*

The Amalekites came out to fight the people of Israel. Joshua and some fighting men went out to meet them in battle while Moses went to the top of a nearby hill. On the hill, Moses raised his hands in the air. As he did, the battle went in favor of the Israelites. But it was a long, hard battle and his hands would fall. If they fell, the battle went towards the Amalekites. So, Aaron and Hur helped to hold Moses' arms up when they began to fall and had him sit on a rock as the battle raged on. Israel prevailed victorious.

THAT is what the church is supposed to look like. When people have a battle going on in their lives, we are the ones who are supposed to hold them up and encourage them to rest upon the rock—Jesus. We do that by being exactly what we've been called to be—Christians. We bring light to the darkness in people's lives. Anyone sitting in a pew at your congregation could have a faith that is hanging on by threads—how you treat them could by the final cut. Or your kind words or gesture could be what gives them faith in having faith.

I once spoke to someone who was contemplating leaving the church based on how she had been treated. She loved God but wasn't crazy about the church. She said, "Why is it I can find compassion and understanding in a bar…but I can't find it in the church?" She had gone through a lot, and I mean A LOT, yet when she turned to the people who were supposed to help her, she found closed doors, rumors, and name calling. "I'm thinking about walking away…."

My wife and I, in our younger years, loved to do mud run obstacle course races. A five-kilometer race through rugged terrain filled with mud and different obstacles every few hundred yards or so. (Google Spartan Races and you'll get the idea). Man, they were tough. You were exhausted from the get-go. Within the first 100 yards, you're covered in mud. Thick mud. Mud that would suck your shoes off if you weren't careful. Then you'd come to some obstacle that made you question your life choices. Cargo nets, monkey bars, rope climbs, tire flips, sandbag carry, and low crawls under barbed wire. Yet no matter what obstacle we came to, there was always someone in the mud with us willing to help. Each obstacle was a challenge, but the last obstacle…that was something else entirely. It was a large, warped wall, about 25 feet high. At the top, there was a small piece of rope hanging down just to give you a little hope that you could conquer it. Your job was to run up the slick wall, grab the rope and get onto the platform. Piece of donut…

Now remember, you've just ran 4.9 kilometers through tough terrain. You're tired, you're wet, you're covered in mud, and now you must find the strength to get up a curved wall that is covered in slippery mud. Here is where your help comes from. It's not from the people standing on the side lines—it's the people beside you and the people who have already conquered it. The people who are in the mud with you.

If you can grab that rope, the people at the top will pull you up to the top. If you couldn't reach the rope, people at the bottom would lay down on the ramp and build a human ladder. Then you'd climb up them and they'd push you to the rope. You're tired, you're wet, you're covered in mud, you're cold—yet you know the people beside you are just as dirty and gross as you are—and they're going to help you conquer that obstacle.

The thought of quitting mid-race was ever-present in my mind, but people I didn't even know helped me get through it. That is how we should be in the church. You can be the difference in someone's life. A simple hug can be the catalyst that lights the fire in someone's soul and brings him closer to Jesus. A "we miss you" could bring the prodigal back. The Shunammite woman (2 Kings 4) showed kindness to Elisha by just giving him food and a place to lay his head on his journey. Elisha would later bring her son back to life. What would have happened if she had never shown those simple acts of kindness?

One of my favorite Bible stories is in Mark 2. Jesus is in Capernaum and a large crowd gathers at the house. Four friends bring their paralyzed friend to be healed by Jesus, but due to the large crowd, they can't get inside. They climb on top of the house, make a hole, and lower the friend down to Jesus to be healed. Usually when I hear this story, I'm reminded of the importance of having friends who would carry me to Jesus. I'd rather have four good friends who would carry me to the feet of Jesus than eight friends who want to carry me to a bar—because I know that Jesus can heal my pain. The bar will try to drown my sorrows—and my sorrows are really good swimmers.

Let's look at it from a different angle. It is important to have the right friends. No denying that fact. BUT—it is important to BE the friend that carries the paralyzed friend (or stranger) to Jesus. You can be that person. If you wear the name of Christ, it should be your privilege. No matter what paralyzes them—be it anger, fear, doubt, alcohol, drugs, pornography, whatever—you need to be the kind of friend who would carry that person to Jesus. So many people distrust the police because of the actions of a few. May we never be one of those few who cause someone to distrust God and walk away from the church. You can be the one that pulls them up onto the platform, or the one who cuts the few strands they're hanging onto and send them crashing to the bottom. Choose kindness. You never know what someone is going through. May God always be merciful when we fail to show the love of Jesus.

Jesus warned that there would be "false prophets, who come to you in sheep's clothing, but inwardly they are ravenous wolves" (Matthew 7:15). You know who those "wolves" are today? It's me when I wear my "Jesus is Lord" t-shirt and fail to show love to that kid in church (you know the one I'm talking about). It's me when I wear my WWJD bracelet and yet gossip about how a certain family can't get to church on time. I mean, really, how hard is it to get all those kids ready and get to church so they don't interrupt the service? It's me when I spread rumors about what may or may not have happened at church camp that one summer. It's me when I spend all my time memorizing the Scriptures and spend no time applying them in my life. It's me when love is absent in my life.

Paul put it this way:

> *Though I speak with the tongues of men and of angels, but have not love, I have become sounding brass or a clanging cymbal. And though I have the gift of prophecy, and understand all mysteries and all knowledge, and though I have all faith, so that I could remove mountains, but have not love, I am nothing. And though I bestow all my goods to feed the poor, and though I give my body to be burned, but have not love, it profits me nothing* (1 Corinthians 13:1-3).

You can go to church, read your Bible, sing the songs, give all your money, and do all the "things" Christians are supposed to do, but if you don't have love, Paul said you're nothing. You're a wolf....

In Matthew 25, Jesus says that He is going to come back to separate His sheep from everyone else at the judgment. The sheep will hear, "Then the King will say to those on His right hand, 'Come, you blessed of My Father, inherit the kingdom prepared for you from the foundation of the world" (vs. 34). Everyone else will hear "Depart from Me, you cursed, into the everlasting fire prepared for the devil and his angels" (vs. 41). Which will you hear? Are you one of His sheep? Or are you just pretending to be a sheep but really you are a wolf?

WORDS TO WEIGH

1. When you visit a congregation, and no one greets you, how do you feel when you leave? What impact does that have on how you treat visitors or new members at your congregation?

2. Why is it hard for us to be open and honest with our brothers and sisters in Christ regarding our daily struggles in our life? Why do we wear fake masks when we come to the assembly and just pretend everything is okay when inside we're falling apart? What does the Bible say to do instead? Find a few verses that tell us.

3. What steps can you take to help change that attitude in your congregation? Discuss with a friend and make a plan!

4. How does focusing on being the friend who brings someone to Jesus help us better deal with the wolves we might run into in the church?

5. What benefit is there in having two people (Aaron and Hur) in helping someone who is weary and needing strength? Name someone who will be Aaron or Hur with you and then find someone who feels like Moses to support!

CH. 8
Checking for Prints

A call came in late one night from a frantic wife claiming her veteran husband was having an episode of PTSD and was destroying the house. Several officers responded to the residence but did not get there before the husband ran out the back door and into a large, wooded section of the neighborhood. In speaking with the wife, the officers learned that the husband left possibly armed with his handgun and was claiming that he going to go kill "the enemy." Who the enemy was, no one knew. More officers were requested to the scene to set up a perimeter so they could locate the husband.

This husband had extensive training from his military career and had done several tours overseas. He was a Navy Seal, Army Ranger, Marine Scout Sniper, and the Terminator all in one. This guy would give Chuck Norris a run for his money. He was legit. And he was having a severe PTSD episode while running through the woods with his boom stick. This was about as intense a situation as you could imagine.

The sergeant began to disperse his units to different areas around the wooded area to try to contain him while a negotiator began calling the man's cell phone. The man would only talk for a moment and then hang up. This went on for the better part of 30 minutes until finally, the man walked out of the woods and surrendered peacefully.

The sergeant, an old war dog himself, took the time to have some one-on-one conversations with the husband about what he'd been going through and how the police department could get him some help. Well, during his talks, the sergeant learned some very disturbing news.

The man told him how he had been looking for an avenue to slip through our perimeter. He didn't want to get into a shootout with the police, but he would have if he felt it necessary. He was extremely well trained with real-world experience to back it up. He could have easily sniped an unsuspecting officer not on his A game. And he found such an officer. As he was maneuvering through the brush, the man saw his opportunity to make an escape. He noticed a patrol car parked by an intersection with the officer sitting in the driver seat. The patrolman was looking down into his lap, and the veteran could see that his face was illuminated by a screen. He inched out of the woods and approached the car from the rear. He was able to get up to the driver side door and see the TikTok videos the officer was watching on his phone. The patrolman was completely unaware of who was standing just two feet away from him. The man could have killed the officer right there. But he didn't. He thought about never being able to see his loved ones again, so, rather than end someone's life, he elected to turn himself in to another officer.

I thought the same thing you're probably thinking. Surely, he wasn't really telling the truth. There was no way, at such a high-risk call, that an officer would just be sitting in his car watching TikTok videos! You're saying that this officer was watching crazy cat videos while Captain America is running through the woods contemplating killing everyone? Is that what you're saying?

"If you don't believe me, check the back of his car. I left my thumb print on his left rear taillight" were his words to the sergeant who hadn't believe him either.

After clearing the scene, the sergeant called the officer to the police department and the two inspected his patrol car. On the left taillight was a fresh crystal-clear thumb print. Right where the man said it would be. The officer was suspended for an Internal Affairs investigation and later fired.

Now that actually happened. No cap! (That means I'm not exaggerating when I tell you something that is hard to believe. I learned that in the high school. Word up!). Now you and I hear about that, and we wonder how an officer could be so careless. How could he, knowing what kind of person was running wild, just sit in his car and play on his phone? My man was a legit, confirmed kills, counter-surveillance extraordinaire, terrorist-hunting, super soldier—and you're just sitting in your car playing on your phone? Are you kidding me? This officer had attended countless hours of training where this very topic was discussed. He had read the news reports of officers constantly being ambushed in their cars. He knew the danger that was out there and maintained this "it won't happen to me" attitude. But it did happen to him, and it almost cost him everything.

What's crazier to me is that so many Christians have the same attitude that officer had. Satan is running all over the place leaving his prints all over their cars, their houses, and THEIR FAMILIES, but they are too busy having their noses in their phones to even notice.

Now, if you'll bear with me for the next few minutes, I'm going to "keep it real" and say some things that might step on a few toes. And if your foot gets smashed, maybe your heart is in the wrong spot. This is too important of a topic not to be discussed. But I'm speaking to me too. Please don't read this thinking I don't have any of these problems. I do. It's a struggle, but we must do better. We must. We must! It's not an option—it's a necessity.

We see it everywhere, don't we? Go sit down at a restaurant and look around. You'll see more families sitting at a table playing on phones than you will see people actually having meaningful conversations. You won't have to drive very far to see other drivers with their noses in their phones. They'll be driving a 3,000-pound missile at 70+ mph and won't be paying any attention to their surroundings because they need to watch a TikTok someone just posted. You go to a family get together and everyone is just sitting around scrolling Facebook. Go to a nearby playground and look at the parents. I guarantee you most of them won't be watching their kids and will be completely absorbed by their phones.

I was speaking in Alabama one year and had the opportunity to go to the space museum. I saw a man sitting on a bench while his kid was playing in an exhibit. He went three minutes straight before looking up from his phone to find his daughter. Three minutes! Anyone could have snatched that girl and been in the parking lot before he even knew she was gone. Everywhere you go, you'll see people completely oblivious to the world around them because they can't or won't take their eyes off that screen.

First Peter 5:8 tells us we must "be sober, be vigilant; because your adversary the devil walks about like a roaring lion, seeking whom he may devour." He's been walking around for thousands of years and he's good at what he does. If you are spending more time on your phone than with your kids—you are failing. Your kids are more important than that picture of spaghetti your neighbor just posted. If you are spending more time on your phone than with your wife/husband—you are failing. We must spend more time with our family than we do with our phones. Strong families take time to build. Personal time. One-on-one kind of time. You only have them for a short time. You can always get a new phone, but you only get so many hours with your family. Put your phone down.

I've been to congregations where parents, in the middle of the worship service, are scrolling Facebook or playing some game while their children are running wild in the pews. Or they might be on their phone while their teen is sitting right next to them. What message are we sending by doing that? What are you teaching your teen if you can't get off your phone for a one-hour worship service? Why did you even bother showing up if all you're going to do is play a game or scroll Facebook? How can you take communion "in remembrance of Me" (Luke 22:19) with your phone out? You can't go back to the cross and really concentrate on everything He did for you with Instagram opened on your screen. I was at a congregation once and saw a pre-teen sitting in the pew playing *Grand Theft Auto* while we were singing praises to God. And his mother let him do it! It's a shame before God. One of the best leaders and biggest influences on my life once told me that when he goes to worship, he likes to leave his phone in the car. He told me that's his time with God and no one will interrupt it. If the president of the United States is calling with a problem that only he can fix, it'll have to wait until the service is over. I personally have gone away from using a Bible app during worship. It was too much of a temptation for me. I would be in the middle of a verse when the notifications would start coming. I just had to know who liked that picture I posted earlier, or I just had to see what so-and-so needed in that text. I went back to using the good ol' fashioned paper Bible. I'm quite fond of the Apologetics Press Defending the Faith study Bible (#ShoutOut—ApologeticsPress.org).

While we are on the topic of cell phones:

Parents—if you are one of those brave souls who trust your offspring to have some device that's connected to the internet, you'd better be checking behind them. "My child would never…." I know, I know… if I've heard it once, I've heard it a million times from parents of kids who did. I could tell you horror stories from now until Jesus comes back and only cover the five years I was working in the high school.

I could tell you about a 15-year-old boy who was randomly messaged by a complete stranger on the Kik App. This stranger pretended to be a female classmate and, in just 10 minutes, convinced this young man to send nude photos. I could tell you about how a 16-year-old girl made a sexual video with her boyfriend, and after they broke up, he used the air-drop function on his iPhone and sent it out in the middle of lunch to some 500 other students. I could tell you about a 14-year-old girl who made a sexual video with her boyfriend, and after they broke up, he posted that video to a pornography website (It took our police department over a month to get the video taken down. By the time it did get taken down, it had been viewed well over one million times). I arrested a 16-year-old boy who followed another boy into the bathroom of the boys' locker room and recorded him using the bathroom—then posted the video on social media. That's just four incidents. In my time at the high school, I spoke to a different set of parents at least twice a week about incidents involving pictures or videos taken and shared on the internet. An overwhelming majority of the parents didn't have a clue what their kids were doing.

The psalmist said, "Unless the Lord build the house, they labor in vain that build" (Psalm 127:1). He goes on to say:

> *Behold, children are a heritage from the Lord,*
> *The fruit of the womb is a reward.*
> *Like arrows in the hand of a warrior,*
> *So are the children of one's youth.*
> *Happy is the man who has his quiver full of them,*
> *They shall not be ashamed,*
> *They shall speak with their enemies in the gate (127:3-5).*

You can picture the idea of the warrior pulling back an arrow and when he has it drawn about as far back as he can muster, he lets it fly towards the enemy. That is how a parent is supposed to be. You train up a child in the way of the Lord (Proverbs 22:6) and aim him in the right direction, so when you let him go into the world, you know the devil will have made a mistake to get in the way. If you haven't been spending this level of personal time with your family, you shouldn't be surprised when those arrows go find a course of their own. You can't be mad at the results you don't get from the work you didn't do.

I was patrolling on a stormy night when I caught a glimpse of a car parked among some trees in the back of one of our parks. The park was closed, and I figured if the car was occupied, they most likely weren't having a Bible study. My partner and I parked our cars a long way off and decide to walk up on them from behind. We make our way through the woods and around to the backside of the car. As we got closer, I could hear the engine was on, but I couldn't see how many people were in the car. Like two stealthy little kittens, we pounced!

To my relief, the two occupants were just watching a movie. But something did stick out as being odd—the girl passenger. She looked way too young to be out this late at night. The man told me he was 22 and had met the girl on a dating app. This was their "first date," and he had picked her up from her house. I asked him how old his "date" was, and he told me she was 18. Ray Charles could have seen this girl wasn't 18.

"How old are you, sweetie?"

"14."

Well, that's awkward. We called the girl's parents who had no idea she had snuck out. I'll give them a pass on that. I was the king of sneaking out of my parents' house without them knowing (sorry Mom and Dad!). The girl admitted to creating a fake profile on a dating app she downloaded onto her iPhone. Her dad allowed us to do a forensic download of her phone which revealed everything she'd been doing on her phone. We got all the photos/videos she had taken (even the deleted ones), all the websites she had been to, all the apps she had downloaded, and all the text messages she's sent/received/deleted. What we found was shocking.

At 14 years old, she had:

- Several fake accounts on numerous dating apps

- Already set up future dates with several grown men

- Several accounts on numerous pornography websites and viewed those sites regularly

- Taken and sent nude photos of herself to unknown people

- Ordered hundreds of dollars of lingerie from various websites

Did I mention she was only 14 years old? Her mom and dad didn't have a clue about any of it. Never crossed their mind that she would be involved in anything like what we had discovered. Nor had they taken any time to check up on her to ensure she wasn't wandering off into a world she didn't need to be. "My child would never...."

My former supervisor had a saying: "I bear the rank and I bear the responsibility." All decisions he made, he owned. If you bear the rank of parent, you bear the responsibility of one. You don't have to be perfect at it; none of us will ever be. Noah wasn't perfect but at least he got his family on the boat (Genesis 7:7). If you make the decision to blindly trust your child with a device with more computing power than what was used to send a man to the moon, you own the consequences. No, you can't protect them from everything this world will throw at them. Nor am I saying lock them in their rooms until they're 18. What I am saying is that you don't want to be in the chairs the parents of the 14-year-old had to sit in while I told them everything their daughter had been doing right under their noses. You don't want to ever think to yourself, "I wish we would have ___."

"But if anyone does not provide for his own, and especially for those of his household, he has denied the faith and is worse than an unbeliever" (1 Timothy 5:8). Have you ever asked, "provide what?" I would suggest that refers to the needs of the family, both physical and spiritual. One must provide food, clothing, etc. but also provide protection against physical forces and spiritual ones. May we always be vigilant in protecting our families from the very behaviors that sent Jesus to the cross. May we be so vigilant in our faith that on the day of judgment, God looks at our lives and sees the thumb print of His Son on our souls.

WORDS TO WEIGH

1. If you are a parent reading this chapter, do you regularly check your child's phone or tech devices? Do you have software or barriers in place to help protect them from things on the internet? If you don't, I encourage you to do some research this week on the different monitoring apps that can aid you in this endeavor. Maybe consider Covenant Eyes®, Qustodio®, Pinwheel®, Bark®, or checking with your service provider about their options.

2. Talk to your children/teens about the dangers that exist in the real world! Don't let your children get blindsided by the dark side of technology.

3. For one week, keep a record of how much you are on your phone (you can use the screen time monitoring on your phone). Does the result surprise you? Make a conscious effort to be present with those around you. What steps will you take to set a better example?

4. What are some things you could do with that time instead that would benefit you (or others!) spiritually? Make a plan to do some of them this week!

CH. 9
"Why You Running?"

It isn't very often you hear your police chief call out on the radio that he's in a foot chase. Sure, I've heard strange things come across the radio, but this was a new one. The chief was coming back from lunch with two detectives and as was their custom, they liked to drive around the city and let the food settle. Ah, the life of being the chief. As they were driving through a neighborhood that was more prone to crime, they happened upon someone throwing a brick through a car window and then snatching a shopping bag from the passenger seat. Hence the foot chase.

The chief gave me updates as the man ran behind a row of houses and started jumping fences. I came into the neighborhood sideways and tried to get ahead of them. My car came to a sliding halt as I slammed it into park a few streets up. I ran behind the houses just in time to see the bad guy high stepping through the shrubs on the outside of the fences. A short distance back was the chief doing his best to keep up. Chief wasn't exactly a "spring chicken." The last call he responded to before becoming the chief was the domestic dispute between Cain and Abel. But he was in the fight and that's all that mattered.

With my new P.F. Flyers laced up tight, I was running faster and jumping higher. Scotty Smalls wasn't kidding—these things worked! Up and over the fence I went, and I was in the chase! He was only 100 feet in front of me and running out of gas. He obviously didn't have any P.F. Flyers. Right as he tired out, here I came with a tackle that was sure to make an NFL highlight reel. Honestly, I'm still surprised no one has made a movie about it yet. Anway…we landed in a briar bush. Rolling around in a briar bush: zero out of five stars. I do not recommend. Apart from that, it was amazing.

I've never really enjoyed running, mainly because I was never good at it. I tried running from the military police when I was in the fourth grade—I didn't make it very far. But that's a story for another chapter in another book. I used to have a t-shirt that said, "Bomb Squad: If you see me running, try and keep up." That summed up my love for running—I only ran if something was about to go kaboom. I didn't start running proficiently until I got into police work. People were going to run, and I was going to chase them. You only have to lose one foot pursuit to realize you never want to lose another one. If you lose a foot pursuit, then (1) the bad guy got away, and (2) your coworkers will never let you forget about how you got smoked. Cops are ruthless when it comes to making fun of each other. Ruthless…

It's funny when I catch someone who just ran from me. The first question is always, "Why you running?" Even if I know why you were running, I'm still going to ask. My favorite response is, "I got warrants" when they don't have any warrants. Or the ol' faithful saying of, "These aren't my pants" always gets me. Why would that be the first words out of your mouth when you get caught? My partner and I chased a guy through a trailer park one night. He ran up the steps of a trailer and broke right through the front door. I tackled him in the living room and the fight was on like Donkey Kong. My partner came in and filled that living room with O.C. spray. He sprayed the walls, the ceiling, the couch, the TV…me! He hit everything BUT the bad guy. We finally got him in custody, and I asked, "Why you running?"

"These aren't my pants!" #Random. He had 100 grams of cocaine in his pocket. Happens more than you would think.

Have you ever considered people who ran in the Bible and why they were running in the first place? Were they running from something or towards something? Consider Jonah, for example. "Now the word of the Lord came to Jonah…saying, 'Arise, go to Nineveh, that great city, and cry out against it; for their wickedness has come up before

Me" (Jonah 1:1-2). "But Jonah arose to flee..." (vs. 3). It took Jonah to verse three to start messing things up.

Now, the Assyrians weren't exactly BFFs with the Jewish people. We can imagine why Jonah didn't want to go preach a message of repentance to them. Maybe some of his friends or family had been killed by them. Think back to a time where you saw a news report of some horrible crime. I mean, h-o-r-r-i-b-l-e. Something that happened that really made your skin crawl and your blood boil with rage. I think of school shootings where elementary school kids were the targets. How someone could go into a school and end the lives of innocent, helpless children is beyond my comprehension. We went to a house one time where a lady left her infant son in the care of her new boyfriend while she ran some errands. She came home to find her baby had bruises all over his body. I'd never seen a baby with so many bruises. The boyfriend was pretty drunk and his story about how the bruises came to be on the baby didn't make sense, so after the investigation was complete, we went to arrest him. Being drunk, he wanted to fight and ended up getting slammed through the kitchen table. Perhaps you think about reports of a serial rapist or some financial crime targeting the elderly. Whatever horrible crime you're thinking about—picture God coming to you and telling you that it is your job to go preach a message of repentance to the one who did the crime and then picture that person receiving God's forgiveness. If that leaves a bad taste in your mouth, you have some idea of how Jonah felt when God told him to go preach to Ninevah. Well, whatever the exact reason was, Jonah ran the opposite direction of where God told him to go and ended up being fish food...kinda.

He preached to the people of Nineveh—and wouldn't you know it—the entire city repented. What should be a cause for celebration turned sour as Jonah became angry over God's gift of forgiveness being bestowed on them that they apparently didn't deserve. At least in Jonah's eyes they didn't deserve it. It reminds me of the time my sister got a boombox for her birthday when she didn't deserve one. Anyway...

"Ah Lord, was not this what I said when I was still in my country? Therefore, I fled previously to Tarshish; for I know that You are a gracious and merciful God, slow to anger and abundant in lovingkindness, One who relents from doing harm" (Jonah 4:2). This is what is called "gaslighting" nowadays. "God, I didn't want to go to Nineveh because I knew how great and how forgiving You are." In the words of a teenage girl from the 90s, "Um, duh!" That was the whole point of your going, Jonah! Because God is who He says He is.

I watched several different documentaries on the serial killer Jeffrey Dahmer. Don't go Googling his story if you are the least bit squeamish. It's rough for me to even read some of the things he did to his victims. It was truly horrific. He made the worst horror movie look like a Saturday morning cartoon. While Jeffrey Dahmer was going through the judicial process, he requested and was given a copy of the Bible. A few phone calls later, enter church of Christ preacher Roy Ratcliff. After some study, Mr. Ratcliff baptized Jeffrey Dahmer in the prison.

As you can imagine, this story would and still does, bring about some strong emotional responses. Now I'm not here to place judgment on whether his conversion was genuine or not. That's well outside the scope of this chapter and my authority to judge. Here is what I do want to point out—the invitation given by God for forgiveness is open for all. Period. It was open to those in Ninevah, it was open for Jeffrey Dahmer, and it is still open for anyone alive today. It is also our job as Christians to go to our Ninevah and bring the good news of forgiveness found in Jesus Christ despite whatever obstacles lie in our path. Why? Because God is who He says He is!

In 2 Kings 5, we read about Naaman, the mighty man of valor who was plagued with the dreaded and incurable disease of leprosy. He came to the door of the prophet Elisha, who gave him instructions on how to be cured. His instructions were peculiar, it's true, but Naaman followed them and his leprosy was cured. To give thanks to Elisha, Naaman tried to bestow a large amount of wealth on Elisha. Elisha refused the gift and Naaman departed. But Gehazi, Elisha's servant had a thought. "...I will RUN after him [Naaman] and take something from him" (2 Kings 5:20). He caught up to Naaman and told him, "My master has sent me, saying, 'Indeed, just now two young men of the sons of the prophets have come to me from the mountains of Ephraim. Please give them a talent of silver and two changes of garments'" (2 Kings 5:22). That was a bold-faced lie if I've ever heard one, and I've heard one or two in my day. When he returned, Gehazi was confronted by Elisha, and Elisha cursed him with leprosy.

People today have a similar idea. They run after money. Gehazi had just witnessed a man miraculously healed by dipping seven times in the Jordan River and still had the audacity to risk his life and soul over a few bags of silver. We have that mindset, don't we? I remember they offered us overtime in December to work an extra six hours on our day off to deter robberies and break-ins. I worked 29 days straight that year chasing the dollar. I wanted to buy my kids the latest and greatest things. On the 29th day of working my wife stopped me with, "When are you going to stop? Your kids miss you." She could have punched me in the nose, and it wouldn't have hurt as badly as I felt knowing I missed out on some memories with my kids chasing some easy overtime. Never again.

The Bible is filled with warnings about running after a dollar. "For the love of money is a root of all kinds of evil" (1 Timothy 6:10). "It is easier for a camel to go through the eye of a needle than for a rich man to enter into the kingdom of God" (Matthew 19:24). Judas betrayed Jesus for a few pieces of silver. The rich young ruler "went away sorrowful" when Jesus told him to sell everything he had and give it to the poor (Mark 10:22). It's not bad to have money—as long as your money doesn't have you.

After the death of Jesus, Mary Magdelene went to visit the tomb of Jesus. Yet when she got there, she found the stone had been rolled away and the tomb was empty. She "ran" (John 20:2) to tell Peter. Then Peter and John "ran together" (John 20:4) to the tomb and found it just as Mary had said. Empty. Only the linen cloth that was used to wrap his body. The text continues, "Then the other disciple, who came to the tomb first, went in also; and he saw and believed. For as yet they did not know the Scripture, that He must rise again from the dead" (John 20:8-9).

Can you imagine what that was like? You have been with Jesus throughout His ministry. You saw the miracles, heard His messages, watched Him be hung on the cross and then buried in the tomb. Then you come running to that empty tomb and while standing there where He was laying, it hits you. You understand what happened. He has risen. How overwhelming that must have been to be standing in the very tomb of Jesus having that realization that He did it! He rose from the dead. They went from a state of grief to pure joy in a moment.

I imagine that feeling was similar to what the prodigal son felt after that long walk home from the far country (Luke 15:11-32). He took his money and went to have a great time. Oh, I'm sure he made plenty of friends, had great food, plenty of drinks, nice clothes. He was living it up. That place was "lit," as the kids these days say. Until the money ran out. The friends really weren't friends. The cups ran dry. The plates were bare. The prodigal found himself feeding pigs and no one would give him anything (vs. 16). He made the hard decision to make the trek back home in hopes of being a lowly servant in his father's house. As he came into view of his father, the text says that his father "ran" to him (vs. 20) and restored him into his house. It was as though he had never left.

God will do the same thing to you. I don't know your situation, your life, your past, what you've done or what you've said. It doesn't really matter. What matters is your heart being open to God's offer. Why you running? Stop living that life in the far country and come home. Come learn to walk by faith (2 Corinthians 5:7) so you too can run the race (1 Corinthians 9:24).

WORDS TO WEIGH

1. Galatians 5:7 says, "You were running well; who hindered you from obeying the truth?" (ESV). Who or what in your life hinders you from fully obeying God? What steps are you going to take to change that?

2. How can we stay focused on our spiritual race and eternal rewards when we have so many temporary distractions in our daily lives?

3. Abraham ran to meet the visitors (Genesis 18:2).

4. Joseph ran from Potiphar's wife (Genesis 39:12).

5. David ran to meet Goliath (1 Samuel 17:48).

6. Jacob ran to meet Esau (Genesis 33:4).

7. Pick one, two, three, or be an overachiever and pick all four. Looking at each account, write down what we should be running toward or away from.

CH. 10
Walking with Milan

I've been playing Cops and Robbers professionally now for over two decades. I started right out of high school at 18 years old. I somehow graduated high school in May and started the police academy that July. I saw the events of 9/11 happen in my junior year of high school while sitting in my Spanish 1 class. We watched the news station every day for the next week. No schoolwork was done. We just sat there in our seats watching the news. I watched as firefighters and police officers work through the day and through the night sifting through the rubble. That was the moment I decided that's what I wanted to do with my life.

I've held a lot of different positions throughout my career. I started as a patrol officer at a local university of about five thousand students. Then I moved on to being a patrol officer with a city police department. I've worked as a traffic officer, school resource officer at a high school, shift supervisor, DUI enforcement officer, and a SWAT operator. Becoming a detective is the only position I haven't held because that sounds so boring. Why? (1) No cool car with flashy lights. (2) No car chases. (3) Generally, you get to a scene after all the chaos is over. (4). No car chases. I want to be in the fast car chasing the bad guys. I want to be in the action right when it happens! Flying a desk Monday–Friday trying to put the clues together and figure out "who done it" is not appealing to me. #Boooooring.

I was working as a school resource officer when my department put out an e-mail about a new position opening soon. It was a K-9 spot. Well color me intrigued! Working with a dog has always interested me, but these spots rarely become available. When they do, they are highly competitive spots. At least that's how it was then. Nowadays,

I know of agencies that will hire brand new officers straight to K-9 positions. But I digress...

After speaking with the boss (my wife) and getting her blessing, I applied for the spot. Four months later, I went to Daytona, Florida, and picked out my partner. He was a one-year-old German Shepherd from Hungary named Milan (pronounced My-Linn) trained in narcotic detection. At the time of this writing, we've been partners now for six years. We've made cases together at the local, state, and federal level. We were called to assist the DEA with a traffic stop of a suspected drug dealer. Milan sniffed around the car, told me he smelled the drugs, and we went spelunking into the car. The drugs we found, even though a rather small amount, led the DEA agent in charge of the case to file for a murder charge on the drug dealer who had been selling pills containing a lethal dose of Fentanyl.

Of all the positions I've held, being a K-9 handler has been my favorite position hands down. I get paid to walk a dog! Every day is a "bring your friend to work" day for me. Now, it is a lot of work. It's not always sunshine and rainbows. For example: the hair. Y'all, my dog sheds! He sheds, and he sheds, and he sheds. When I let him out of his kennel in my back seat, it looks like Cousin It got into a fight with a weed whacker (that was an *Addams Family* reference for you un-cultured people). And it gets everywhere! It's not uncommon to see just big globs of his hair rolling across the floor at my house. His hair has become a condiment at the casa de Zirpolo.

Here is another example. Around 11:00 p.m. every night we work, I make sure to take him out to one of our schools and we go for a nice walk. Usually, it is around a half mile to a mile and a half. Milan will occasionally find water—whether it is a puddle, a pond, or run-off from a school sprinkler—and will stop to try to drink it. I always have to yell at him not to drink that nasty water. It's aggravating because we do this every night! We've been doing this for years and he knows that when we get back to my car, I'm going to pour him a nice, fresh, clean, cold bottle of water into his bowl. He knows it—I do it every night! When we get done walking, he will go and wait by my trunk for me to give him his water. And still, when we go for a walk, he wants to stop along our way and drink some nasty water that could make him sick or give him some parasite that could kill him. "Aggravating as fire," as we say in the South.

Some Christians can be like that in their walk. Well, I say some Christians, but it really happens to all of us, doesn't it? We're on our walk with God and we see that dirty puddle water and think to ourselves, *"That looks delicious." "That looks refreshing."* For us, that might be alcohol, pornography, drugs, cursing, gossip, or lying. Maybe it is some sort of false doctrine, false hope, or selfish desire you have. It's different for each of us. We go over and take a drink, not knowing that what we are ingesting could kill our faith.

Simon the sorcerer was a newly converted Christian when he saw the apostles laying hands on the people (Acts 8:9-21). Simon desired this power and offered Peter money to purchase it. "Your money perish with you because you thought that the gift of God could be purchased with money! You have neither part nor portion in this matter, for your heart is not in the right in the sight of God" (vs. 20-21). Apparently, Simon wanted the power to impart the Holy Spirit to people so he could be looked at as someone of importance. He didn't want the gift so God could be glorified but rather so he could be glorified.

Ananias and Sapphira, the husband-and-wife duo, sold some property that they owned and gave a portion of the proceeds to Peter—lying about the actual price they had received for the property. They had just watched Barnabas and others sell their land, houses, and other possessions and give all the money to the apostles (Acts 4:32-37). Then they sold their property and lied about how much they sold it for. Peter asked the same question I ask myself today: Why? Why lie about it? They could have sold it for $100 and given the apostles $75 as long as they were honest about it. But they lied! It was theirs to sell, and it was their money after they sold it—why lie about it? The answer seems obvious: They wanted to look righteous and holy. They saw that muddy puddle of selfishness and decided to have a drink. It cost them their lives.

Make sure that whomever you decide to walk beside in this life is someone that will encourage you to walk according to God's Word. Someone who isn't afraid to hurt your feelings if it means keeping you on the right path. You don't want a spouse that is ok with you lying to look righteous in front of people. You want a husband or wife that will encourage you to actually be righteous—but for God's glory, not yours. Your spouse should push you to drink the living water that Jesus gives (John 4:13).

Now I love going on walks with Milan. Especially when the weather is nice. A nice 80-degree day, a slight breeze, maybe a light cloud or two—ah, that's the best day to walk. I can put on the "Hey Joe Show" podcast (#ShoutOut—available on Spotify, Apple Music) and just stroll along with my dog and enjoy life. It doesn't take much to motivate me to walk with Milan when the weather is good. But when the weather is less than pleasant, it's harder. But Milan doesn't care about the weather—he wants to walk. Tornados are all around me—he wants to walk. A Category 5 hurricane is coming—he wants to walk. Below freezing temperatures? He wants to walk. So, we walk.

It's easy to be a Christian when the sun is shining and there aren't any clouds in the sky. It's easy to sing "It Is Well with My Soul" when you have money in the bank and your family is healthy. It's easy to want to walk with God when there is food on the table. But what about when the rain comes? Do we still walk with God?

I don't know about you, but I find it hard to say, "Thank you God" when I'm grieving the loss of a friend. It's hard to sing God's praises when the bank accounts are running low, when I have the man flu, or when everything is just going wrong. It's hard! I must remind myself when trouble comes my way and when hard times fall on me, like Peter said, "Lord, to whom shall we go? You have the words of eternal life" (John 6:68).

Look in Mark 12 with me. Starting in verse 41, Jesus tells of a poor widow who came to the treasury and put in two mites. We only know two things about her life: she had very little money, and she lost her husband. Perhaps she had recently lost him. Grieving is hard. Being poor is hard, especially in those times. Yet, even in her situation—being poor and without her husband—she still came to the treasury to praise God with an offering of two mites. She gave God everything she had (vs. 44). Even though the rain was falling in her life, she put on her rain boots and walked with God. May we have that kind of courage and faith.

Consider Job. Job went from living a good life to losing family members, personal property, and his health. All in the blink of an eye. Yet Job said, "Naked I came from my mother's womb, and naked shall I return there. The Lord gave and the Lord has taken away. Blessed be the name of the Lord" (Job 1:21). Job's own wife came to him and told him to "curse God and die" (Job 2:9) and Job replied, "You speak as one of the foolish women speaks. Shall we indeed accept good from God, and shall we not accept adversity?" (2:10). His life had been shattered to pieces, and he was still faithful in his walk with God.

Daniel was thrown into a den of lions for being faithful to God, and instead of abandoning his faith, he prayed to God (Daniel 6). He was literally staring death in the eyes, and he knew the only one who could get him through that nightmare was God!

Paul and Silas, in a Roman prison, sang praises to God (Acts 16). They were in prison—not for stealing, assault, robbery, or murder—but for casting a demon out of a slave girl. And now it was late at night. I imagine they were hungry, cold, uncomfortable, and tired. What did they do? They prayed and sang to God. Paul, how can you pray and sing while you're in prison? I can't believe that the acoustics were as good as our jails today. But he did anyway. He prayed and sang to the God of Heaven—the only one who could bring an earthquake that would allow them to walk out of that prison.

I could go on and on with examples like these. The Bible is full of examples of people who were "going through it" (as we say where I'm from) yet kept their faith in God. It's almost like God knew hard times were going to come our way and we were going to need examples to follow.

I enjoy walking with Milan because I know he is a natural protector. We usually walk at night and the places we walk aren't very well lit. But I know if something comes out of the woods around us, Milan will be the first one in the fight. If a coyote comes out of darkness thinking he's going to eat me—he must get past Milan first. The same is true when you walk with God through life. He's a natural protector. We sing the song in worship "The Battle Belongs to the Lord." The idea behind the song is God is going to fight the battles. Evil coming into your life isn't an attack on you—it's an attack on God, and He'll fight for you.

Paul told Timothy, "But the Lord stood with me and strengthened me, so that the message might be preached fully through me, and that all the Gentiles might hear. Also I was delivered out of the mouth of the lion. And the Lord will deliver me from every evil work and preserve me for His heavenly kingdom. To Him be glory forever and ever. Amen" (2 Timothy 4:17-18). God was with Paul when he was struggling, and he knew He would be with him until Heaven. The same is true for you and me today as we walk with God. "But the Lord is faithful, who will establish you and guard you from the evil one" (2 Thessalonians 3:3).

Am I scared walking at night in a dark place with Milan? Nah. Because we're a team. I know he'll protect me. He'll throw himself in front of me to protect me from anything that would wish me harm. Jesus did the same thing for us. You and I were walking in darkness and headed straight to eternal damnation. But this Jesus came and threw Himself between us and an eternity apart from God by hanging on a cross over 2,000 years ago. He did that so you and I could have the hope of Heaven. He did it so you and I could have a home with Him.

It's interesting that when I leave home without Milan, he has the same reaction when I come back. I can be gone for five seconds or five days: He always has the same reaction—pure joy. He jumps around, spins in circles, and just goes bonkers. I wonder if God doesn't have that same level of joy when we come home to Him.

Luke 15:7 says there is more Heaven over one sinner that repents than over 99 righteous than don't need repentance.

Let's go for a walk.

Photo: My K9 partner Milan and me

WORDS TO WEIGH

1. What "dirty puddles" are attractive to you? List some verses that will help you not drink from those but instead drink from the Living Water (John 4).

2. We see the implications of what can happen when you attach yourself to the wrong person. Let's apply that to friendship. What kind of friend and company does the Bible say you should keep? What can happen if we have more friends outside of the church than in it? How do we go about finding the company that the Bible describes?

3. If you are single or dating, what are some Scriptures that describe what you should look for in a future spouse? Make a list! How might finding someone like that biblical description help you in your Christian walk and life?

4. If you are married, what are some Scriptures that tell you what kind of wife/husband you should be? Are you those things? Find one you struggle with and make a commitment to be that to your spouse.

5. Have you ever faced a difficult time in your life? How did you handle it? The company we keep will push us closer to God or pull us further away during these times. Find people who will pray when you can't and hold you up when you can't stand. Write down some Scriptures to help you build your faith for when the storms of life rage.

CH. 11
Four Things
I Remember

The high school was on spring break, so I was back on road patrol. For some reason, the powers that be felt that I didn't deserve a free week off for being a resource officer. I dealt with those little angels for seven months. I felt like I had earned a vacation, but alas, the boss denied it. The sergeant on duty asked me to go deliver something to a store around the corner. I remember pulling up to one of our red lights that had two left-turn lanes. If I had made one left turn here, I had made a million. I always got in the lefthand left-turn lane. Always. Don't ask me why; I don't know. Maybe I'm a creature of habit. But that day, I didn't go to the left one—I got in the righthand left turn lane.

The tires of my car had just stopped rolling when something in my rear-view mirror caught my eye. A large red Ford Explorer was approaching me from behind and was coming in fast. Now, I've been trained in speed detection. I can tell how fast a car is going just by looking at it and be within five miles per hour. This SUV was going around 45 miles per hour, and he wasn't slowing down. Even if he slammed on the brakes, I knew he wouldn't be able to stop before he plowed into me. All I could do was brace for impact.

Just before he got to me, the driver snatched the car to the left and annihilated a Cadillac sedan that was right beside me. A full impact without slowing down. He hit the Cadillac so hard that it was thrown into an old Chevrolet Blazer in front of it. The Blazer jumped forward and hit a Toyota in front of it! Instant chaos ensues.

I called for back-up units, EMS, and fire units to respond. Several people were injured. The driver of the Toyota had just been cleared to drive after having back surgery. The driver of the Blazer had been leaning down to grab something off the floorboard when the impact happened. His head smacked into the dash causing a large laceration across his face. Every window in the Cadillac shattered upon impact. The passenger had glass all over her. She had cuts all over her face. A bystander placed a towel over her head to try and stop the bleeding. I got to the driver of the Cadillac, and although he looked okay physically, he wasn't doing well internally.

EMS got on scene as fast as they could but despite their best efforts, the driver died before they could get him to a hospital. What about the driver of the Ford? He was fine. Not so much as a scratch on him. He had been texting and driving. As soon as he looked up from his phone, he saw my car. Then in a panic, he snatched the wheel left and struck the Cadillac. He would later be charged with involuntary manslaughter and sent to prison.

When I look back on that afternoon, there are four things I remember specifically about that accident:

1. **The smell.** When handling an accident, you smell a lot of things you don't normally smell. The air bag dust. The oil, gasoline, and radiator fluid. The smell of the oil dry being poured on the fluids. The diesel exhaust from the ambulance and the fire trucks. If I close my eyes, I can still smell all of them.

2. **The sounds.** When two vehicles collide, they make a unique smacking sound. I don't have to see an accident to know one happened. I just have to hear that sound. I remember hearing the crying and the screams of pain. I remember hearing the sirens in the distance knowing that help was coming. If I close my eyes, I can still hear them all.

3. **The chaos.** It was complete pandemonium. There were car parts everywhere. Bystanders were coming out of the woodwork to see what had happened. Some were trying to help while others were trying to take videos. EMS was scrambling trying to prioritize who to help first. Traffic was instantly congested. It was a mess.

4. **The regret.** Can you imagine how the texting driver felt as he looked around at the mess he made?

What if God would let you and me experience Hell for just a few seconds? What if God would let us take our human bodies past the judgment scene and into the fire? If He would peel back the layers of our world and let us just peer into the voids of Hell just to experience what it would be like to be there? What would you take from such an experience? How would it impact your life? What would you remember? I would suggest that there are at least four things you would remember.

1. **The smell.** Have you ever considered what Hell would smell like to a human nose? There isn't a biblical reference to the smell of Hell, but I would imagine that if we could smell it, it would be one of the foulest assaults on your nose that you've ever experience. The smell of an endless sea of rotting souls burning. I don't know what a soul burning smells like, but I do know what a burnt body smells like.

   I responded to an accident on our interstate where a semi-truck had pinned a car against the guard rail. The semi-truck's gas tank exploded covering the car with liquid fire. The driver of the car was able to get out of the car, but his wife couldn't. She was trapped and burned alive. I don't know if you have ever smelled anything like that, and I pray you never have to, but it is the worst smell imaginable. I don't have words to accurately describe it for you. It is just the worst.

I picture that Hell would have that kind of smell. The worst kind. A smell that causes your eyes to snap shut and your head to just jerk back in retreat.

2. **The sounds.** What would your ears hear if you could listen into the depths of Hell? Now for this, the Bible does give us some insight! In explaining the parable of the wheat and tares, Jesus says the tares (those who practice lawlessness) will be cast into the furnace of fire where, "There will be wailing and gnashing of teeth" (Matthew 13:42).

I've been to scenes where I've heard the screams of gunshot victims. I've heard the screams of families who have unexpectedly lost a loved one. They all scream for the same reason. They want the pain to not exist. That's the kind of sound you would hear in Hell. I imagine those would drown out any other sounds found there. Everyone just wanting the pain to end, but it doesn't. And it never will.

3. **The chaos.** Try to let your finite mind rap around the infinite notion of a massive ocean of fire with a countless amount of people drowning. And every soul there is fighting the one beside him to try and get to the top for a breath of fresh air. But there is no top, and there isn't any fresh air. They are all helplessly clawing at each other to try and find some relief. But no relief is coming. "The devil, who deceived them, was cast into the lake of fire and brimstone where the beast and the false prophet are. And they will be tormented day and night forever and ever" (Revelation 20:10).

4. **Regret.** You would regret looking into Hell because it would be one of those things you wish you could just un-see. But you would also remember seeing souls in that place that you

could have talked to about Jesus but didn't—your friends, your neighbors, or your family members. You could have been the one to say or do something that would have changed their mind and brought them to Christ but didn't. You would see those people and the weight of the regret of what you never said would stay at the forefront of your mind.

You would have a regret like what the rich man experienced in Luke 16. The rich man died and went to Hades. And as soon as his eyes opened in Hades in torment, he was filled with instant regret. He wanted Abraham to send Lazarus back to warn his brothers. Why? Because they were living life just as he did and he knew that if they didn't change their path, Hell would be their destination also. Now, being there, the rich man had to live with his decision for all eternity.

Now, what if God would permit you and me to lift our heads and poke them through the floor of Heaven? What if He would allow us just to bypass judgment and gaze into Heaven for just a few seconds? What would you remember from such an experience? Four things I think you would never forget:

1. **The smell.** There isn't a biblical reference for this, but can you imagine what Heaven would smell like to an earthly nose? May I suggest that it smells like home? My good friend John Farber convinced me to join him on a mission trip with Latin American Missions (lam.forrestpark.org—another shameless plug) to Nicaragua. I couldn't find Nicaragua on a map, but I said yes anyway. We spent a week in Nicaragua on a medical campaign and of all the memories I have of Nicaragua, I can vividly remember the smell. It wasn't bad. It was just Nicaragua. But let me tell you, when I landed in Texas on my way home and I stepped off that plane in God's country, I knew by the first sniff that I was home. Have you ever gone away from home, and you

know right as you walk through the door that you're home just by the smell? I picture that is what Heaven smells like—home.

2. **The sound.** Let your brain run wild and picture the kind of sounds you'd hear in Heaven! I get goose bumps just writing about it.

I think of the singing in Heaven. I love some good church singing! There is nothing better than a good crowd on Sunday and everyone just singing out to God. We attend Y.E.S. (Youth Enrichment Seminar—yes.forrestpark.org—shameless plug again) in Valdosta, Georgia, every year. Around 600 people in attendance and the singing is phenomenal! I've been to Polishing the Pulpit in Sevierville, Tennessee, a few times. Several thousand Christians in attendance all singing praises to God all together will give you a taste of what Heaven will be like. "And they sang a new song…" (Revelation 5:9).

You'd get to hear Jesus welcoming those who lived their lives in accordance to His commands. You'd get to hear Jesus tell someone, "Well done, good and faithful servant…" (Matthew 25:23). How would you feel hearing the voice of the Son of God?

3. **The peace.**

And I heard a loud voice from heaven saying, "Behold, the tabernacle of God is with men, and He will dwell with them, and they shall be His people. God Himself will be with them and be their God. And God will wipe away every tear from their eyes; there shall be no more death, nor sorrow, nor crying. There shall be no more pain, for the former things have passed away." Then He who sat on the throne said, "Behold, I make all things new." And He said to me, "Write, for these words are true and faithful" (Revelation 21:3-5).

All the troubles that this world brings won't be in Heaven. No pain. No tears. No regrets. No sadness. None of them. It's for us to imagine, isn't it? Because we're used to having pain and difficulties in our life. But in Heaven, there isn't any. It's just peace.

4. **The Value.** You'd remember that Heaven was worth all the trials that you went through. Paul said, "For I consider that the sufferings of this present time are not worthy to be compared with the glory which shall be revealed in us" (Romans 8:18). When you left your old life, became a Christian, and all your friends quit being your friends—Heaven will be worth it. When you stopped doing drugs and went through all those times where you wanted another hit—Heaven will be worth it. Whatever life throws at you, being a Christian is worth it because Heaven will be worth it.

If you were keeping count, you know I only told you three of the things I remember about that accident. Here is number four. After everything settled down and the wreck was cleaned up, it hit me. The guilt. Some call it survivor's guilt. I just knew deep down that I should have been the car that got hit. I should have gone into the lane I always got in and I should have been the car the Ford struck. It should have been me. That man shouldn't have died that day; it should have been me. Years later, even while writing this chapter, I still feel the same way. It should have been me. I try and understand why some things happen, and my mind just starts racing trying to find an answer. I always come back to what, at least to me, feels true: It should have been me.

It should have been me on that cross. It should have been you. But it wasn't. Jesus came here and lived a lowly life and bore the sinners' cross so you and I could live. He saw death coming straight at us and He took the hit so you and I could live. He did it so you and I could have our sins forgiven. Then when we get to the judgment scene to answer for how we lived, He won't have to look at us and say, "I never knew you, depart from Me" (Matthew 7:23). Instead, He'll say, "Hey, I remember you...."

WORDS TO WEIGH

1. What are four reasons you want to go to Heaven?

2. Write down four Bible verses that help you stay focused on Heaven.

3. Imagine God would allow you to speak to anyone in Paradise right now. Who would it be and what four things would you ask him/her about Paradise?

4. Now choose someone from Tartarus. What four things would you ask him/her?

CH. 12
Life Is Like
That Sometimes

In the summer of 2010, my good friend's son passed away. He was born with cerebral palsy among other things, and even though he wasn't expected to survive very long, he lived for almost 20 years. While the funeral arrangements were being made, our chief of police at the time informed everyone that if we wished to bring our spouses to the funeral, they could ride with us in our patrol cars. Understand, that's a pretty rare occurrence where I work, but this was a special occasion and the chief wanted to bring as much support to this officer and his family as he was able to muster.

My wife was around five or six months pregnant with our first child at the time while simultaneously working as the head-honcho of a retail store at an outlet mall. Basically, she was Superwoman. The day of the funeral came, and my superhero wife was working. I called and told her I was on the way to pick her up, but much to my dismay, her job was completely swamped with customers. There was no way she was going to be able to get off.

"Just leave. The store will survive without you," I pleaded. She couldn't do it. I got heated—I won't lie. The whiny kid came out because I didn't get what I wanted. But my wife, who doesn't put up with foolishness, put me in my place and sent me off to the funeral. It was as horrible as you would expect it to be. It was great being able to support my friend in his time of grief, but I was so uncomfortable being there, especially without my boo.

You ever notice that sometimes things don't work out the way you want them to work out? You make all these grandiose plans and then none of them happen. Dads, have you ever planned a family vacation? "We're leaving at 8 a.m. sharp!" And at 11:30 a.m. you're finally walking out the door, right? Then as you start beating the time on the GPS (you know what I mean…it's a race!) the youngest of your three boys has an upset tummy and projectile vomits (you know what I mean) all over himself. But you're in the mountains with nowhere to pull over. And when you finally find a spot to pull over, you have nothing to clean him with, so you use one of your shirts to get the job done. The sacrificing of your shirt is only acceptable because he's the baby of the group and you wouldn't have done it for the middle child. ☺ Then you get to the hotel that you spent three mortgage payments on, and the bed isn't comfy. Your oldest wakes up the next day with the flu. Vacation canceled. That wasn't a personal experience or anything…purely hypothetical. Sometimes things just don't go as we planned, but it isn't always for the worst.

After the death of Rachel, Jacob and his sons settled in the land of Canaan. Joseph, being his father's favorite son, was given a coat of many colors and began having dreams about how everyone will bow down to him. But his brothers had other plans. They betrayed Joseph, left him in a pit, and then sold him into slavery for a few pieces of silver (Genesis 37). The Ishmaelites who bought him then take him to Egypt where he is sold again. This time it was to a captain named Potiphar. Some time later, Potiphar's wife made some false accusations against Joseph, and he was thrown in prison (Genesis 39). I can picture Joseph sitting on that floor in the prison thinking to himself, *"This is not working out the way I had thought would."* In the span of just four chapters, Joseph went from "Everyone will bow to me" to "How did I end up in prison?"

Sometimes things just don't go the way we plan them to go. But it isn't always for the worst. That prison wasn't where Joseph's story ended. It was the launching pad for his rise into the second highest position in Egypt. He became second only to the Pharoah and saved countless people by his actions. The Hebrew writer encourages his reader to "lay aside every weight, and the sin which so easily ensnares us, and let us run with endurance the race that is set before us, looking unto Jesus, the author and finisher of our faith, who for the joy that was set before Him endured the cross, despising the shame, and has sat down at the right hand of the throne of God" (Hebrews 12:1-2). There is an endurance theme in the New Testament.

"Lay aside every weight." That means, sometimes things aren't going to go the way you thought it should. Sometimes it is going to hurt. It's not going to be fun. It is going to be lonely. Sometimes you are going to feel like your feet are made of concrete and you aren't sure how you are going to take another step. You must dig deep and fight with everything that is in you to keep going. Life may not be going as you planned, but you have to keep your eye fixed on Jesus because that is who we are running towards.

In 2 Corinthians 11, Paul makes a list of all the things he went through during his travels. Take a gander starting at verse 24,

> *From the Jews five times I received forty stripes minus one. Three times I was beaten with rods; once I was stoned; three times I was shipwrecked; a night and a day I have been in the deep; in journeys often, in perils of waters, in perils of robbers, in perils of my own countrymen, in perils of the Gentiles, in perils in the city, in perils in the wilderness, in perils in the sea, in perils among false brethren; in weariness and toil, in sleeplessness often, in hunger and thirst, in fastings often, in cold and nakedness… (2 Corinthians 11:24-27).*

You think at any time during those beatings, shipwrecks, robberies, sleepless nights being hungry and thirsty that he ever had a thought that life wasn't going the way he had planned it? In chapter 12 he goes on to say that he received a "thorn in the flesh" (vs. 7) that he asked God on three occasions to remove from him and God denied his request. Paul said, "Therefore most gladly I will rather boast in my infirmities, that the power of Christ may rest upon me. Therefore I take pleasure in infirmities, in reproaches, in needs, in persecutions, in distresses, for Christ's sake. For when I am weak, then I am strong" (2 Corinthians 12:9-10). Life didn't go as Paul had planned it, but that was okay—because he trusted God.

That's why I started writing. I had been in some shipwrecks in my life, and I wasn't sure I would be able to swim my way out of them. My wife encouraged me to start writing. "You can either let God use what you've seen, or you can let the devil use it," she said. That's why I wrote these chapters. Life wasn't going the way I had planned it. Maybe that's why this book is in your hands.

After my friend's son's funeral was over and I said my goodbyes, I made my way back home via the interstate. I traveled through our neighboring county and came upon a car that had blown a tire and crashed into the guard rail. The vehicle was blocking the left lane so I, being the superhero I am, turned on the flashy blues and called in the accident.

The officer arrived and told me I can go. He had another officer coming to assist so I didn't have to stay. "I'll stay until he gets here. Ya know…just in case." The officer gathered the information from the driver and sat back in his car to file a report on his MDT (mobile data terminal—a fancy name for a computer). I was standing at his window just having some small chat and watching the traffic crawl by when I caught a yellow blur in the corner of my eye. I looked and saw it was a bright yellow Chevrolet Monte Carlo barreling down on us. Everyone on the interstate but this guy saw we had the lane blocked apparently. I yelled for the officer to watch out as I went jumping over the guard rail to avoid the impending collision. The Monte Carlo never touched the brakes and plowed into the back of the officer's patrol car at 60 miles an hour. The patrol car launched forward and into the back of my patrol car, pushing my trunk into my back seat.

I rushed back to the officer and found him with a severe head injury. His MDT had snapped off its post and struck him in the forehead. The driver of Monte Carlo was also in a lot of pain. I reached into the officer's car and called for assistance on his radio. I probably sounded like a twelve-year girl at a Justin Bieber concert because I was screaming for help. Four state troopers, three patrol officers, a corporal, a sergeant, two lieutenants, a captain, an entire forensics unit, and their traffic team of five officers responded. Both the driver of the Monte Carlo and the patrol officer were transported to a hospital for their injuries. The patrol officer was never able to work in police work again.

If my wife's job hadn't become super busy that day and she had been able to leave with me, she would have been in the front seat of my patrol car when that accident took place. If she had been, she and my unborn son could have been seriously injured. Thank God life doesn't always go the way we plan it to go.

I remember watching a movie where a philosophical question is asked: Why do hot dogs come in packages of ten, but hot dog buns come in packages of eight? At the end of the movie, one of the main characters answers it like this: Life doesn't always turn out the way we think it should, so be content with what you have, and besides, you can always grab a hot dog.

But since this is a book written by a cop—I say you can always grab a donut.

WORDS TO WEIGH

1. Think of a time when something didn't go your way. Can you look back and see any good or blessings that came from it? Take time to thank God for those unexpected blessings.

2. How might trusting God in the unexpectedness of life help us find peace? Find Scriptures that tell about the peace we find in Christ.

3. How did Joseph respond to all the bad that had happened to him? When his brothers asked for forgiveness, what was his reply (Genesis 50:20)? How does considering troubles from an eternal perspective help us keep on when life is hard?

CH. 13
Finding Contentment

In one of the more—shall we say—lively times in my career, I found myself in the office of one of the higher-ranking members of the department. I wasn't in trouble, but we were engaged in what one might call "intense fellowship" over differing opinions. Alright, we were having a knock-down, drag-out argument. He would let an arrow fly and like Serena Willams, I'd send it flying right back. Think Forrest Gump playing ping-pong in the Olympics against the Chinese, but with more yelling.

Oddly enough, toward the end of it he mentioned that he was upset because I never took his advice to put in for a promotion. Younger and less experienced officers who had been hired after me had already been promoted up past me. I didn't mind; I was content where I was doing what I did. I was happy being a low-level street goon. I didn't have to babysit the new guys or answer to the boss as to why that less-than-stellar officer did whatever he or she did. I didn't have to deal with politics from city hall. Yes, contrary to what they say, city halls looooove to be involved in the comings and goings of police department business. I've seen cases get dismissed because of who the defendant knew at city hall. But being where I was—on the lower end of the totem pole—I didn't have to deal with all that foolishness. And I let it be known in that meeting that I was just here to be a goon, and I didn't want to do anything else.

"Jon, I look at your career and notice you've been here some time. And I look at all the good you could have done and all the people you could have trained if you would have put in for promotions and I look at you now and just think, 'What a waste.'"

You know, I've been called a lot of things in my years. A lot. I usually get insulted by one person or another daily. Comes with the territory. "It's the cost of doing business" is what my old major used to tell me. I've been cursed at by the worst of the worst. I've been cursed at by people on their way to a worship service. I've probably forgotten more than I remember about what some people call me. Yet, I had never been called a waste that I can remember. I know I haven't been called a waste by anyone in my command staff until that day.

Let me tell you—that one stung. It has stuck with me ever since he said it. It came from a man who claimed to have a Christian faith. I think that made it a little worse. I, like you I imagine, felt like surely no Christian would call another one a waste merely over a differing opinion. I was wrong. I don't think there are any biblical issues with getting promoted at work or moving up the corporate ladder as long as your Christian principals are kept at the forefront of your ambition. I don't think there is anything wrong, per se, with wanting to have a large bank account or nice things—as long as your focus stays on Heaven and you can find contentment where you are.

Ah contentment. Such a fun topic to talk about in America, the land of opportunity. Where you can be dead broke one day and Jeff Bezos the next with just a simple idea. It is highly encouraged in this country to chase what we call the American Dream. You need the big house, nice cars, flashy clothes, and so forth. You need to get that promotion or your career is a waste. If you don't buy your kid the nicest phone for her birthday—you're a terrible parent. Your 16-year-old needs that brand-new Camaro SS for his birthday. After all, little Tommy down the road got a new car from his parents and if your little Suzie doesn't get one, you have failed as a parent. A "waste" if you will….

When I look back at my marriage, some of the best times we had were when we first got married. We didn't have two nickels to rub together. We bought our townhome by ourselves and just figured it out. For the first few months, the only thing in that house was an old pull-out couch my mom gave us, a big screen projection TV on wheels my dad bought me for graduating high school, and an Xbox 360. That was it. We were broke. But those were the good ol' days and some of our happiest. We were content.

Paul, after telling the Philippians to always think on the good and righteous things, stated that he had learned to be content in whatever circumstance he was in (Philippians 4:11). He had been wealthy; he had been poor. He had days where his stomach would be full to the brim, and he had days when he was hungry. Yet whatever the case, Paul proclaimed that he could "do all things through Christ" who strengthened him (Philippians 4:13).

Here was my problem; maybe you can relate then we can figure this out together. My problem was I always wanted more. If I had $20, I wanted $21. If I had one video game, I needed two, and so on. When I was in high school, I had one of the sweetest cars ever known. A 2003 Toyota Celica. It was silver and came equipped with a sunroof, CD player, automatic windows, and pure excellence. You young guns don't know it, but those weren't standard in all cars back in the day. You had to pay extra cheddar for the automatic windows.

Then, as a less-than-intelligent teenager does, I needed to add some accessories. I needed a new sound system. I added an in-dash TV player connected to two Kicker 12" subs in the trunk. I needed newer, flashier wheels, and an exhaust. Because…reasons. I added red undercarriage lights under the frame. We tinkered under the hood a little and added stuff like a cold air intake. Listen—*The Fast and the Furious* came out two years prior and this was all the rage—stop with your judgments. The point is, I spent more time adding to the car and fixing it rather than just enjoying the fact that I had a car. We can get caught up in our stuff or chasing promotions, can't we? It's very easy to do. Learning how to be content is a long, slow, painful journey. I didn't really comprehend it until I went to Nicaragua in the early 2010s. While there doing mission work with a newly planted congregation, my team journeyed into the mountains to let people know about our campaign. A mile or so up into the mountains, we came across a young lady at a well. She was drawing water using a small bucket attached to some ragged rope trying to fill up her five-gallon bucket. Through our translator we learned that every day she walks two miles down the mountain to fill her bucket just to walk two miles back up the mountain back to her home. This water was for cooking and cleaning. And she did it every day. Culture shock had set in. We asked if we could help her draw some water, but she refused. She was scared we would drop her rope into the well and then she wouldn't have any water for her family.

When we got back to the village, a local fire truck was at our compound filling a large water tank so we could have some water. As they were discharging their hose, the village came out in droves with five-gallon buckets so the water from the hose wouldn't go to waste. It was rather life-changing to see as I came from a place where I could fill a glass of water from my fridge, take a sip, and then just dump the rest down the drain. I came home from Nicaragua with a different perspective—I found contentment with what I had because there are so many people who don't have anything.

Finding contentment is difficult because of all the outside voices we hear in America. Everywhere you go there is someone trying to sell you something. Turn on the radio and you'll probably hear a car salesman at the Toyota dealership trying to convince you that you need a car that isn't as cool as a silver '03 Celica. Or turn on the TV and you'll see the advertisements appealing to your emotions, trying to convince you that what you have isn't enough. You deserve x, y, and *z* because you worked hard and blah, blah, blah. Or it could be your boss at work trying to get you to take a position that requires more time away from your family and church services in exchange for a little more cheddar. We've all been there.

Then the feelings of inadequacy compound the discontent when you are made to feel "less than" if you don't break the bank to get whatever it is that someone is trying to sell to you. Don't you want what is best for your kids? Don't you want what is best for your family? Well, if you want to be father of the year, you need to get this—whatever this is. It is completely false, but we are made to feel that way.

Notice that Paul told the Philippians that he had to "learn" to be content. Read that again. Paul had to learn to be content. That means there is a process involved. You can't go to sleep and learn contentment through osmosis. It means you have to go through some stuff. You have to be put in situations where contentment becomes an end goal. Paul said he had learned contentment, and he learned by being in places at times where he was hungry, full, with plenty, with nothing and so on. It was in those times that he learned contentment. And through learning contentment, he reaffirmed one of the most popular verses quoted throughout the world today: "I can do all things through Christ who strengthens me" (Philippians 4:13).

In the 2006 movie *Rocky Balboa*, Rocky is giving a speech to his son about being his own man. (The director had offered me a stunt double position for Sylvester Stallone, but I was too busy. Maybe next time.) Anyway…he tells his son about how life is hard and it'll beat you down to your knees if you let it. But you have to be willing to take the hits and keep moving forward. That is how winning is done. Man…I could run a marathon through an Alaskan mountain range after that speech. The same holds true for learning contentment. You must be willing to be in those situations where you get hit. And when you get hit, you have to keep moving forward. That's how learning contentment is done.

Contentment, for me at least, is found in the realization that my identity is in Christ. So, when I am told that I'm a "waste" because I don't want to move up the ladder, I remind myself of whose I am—Christ's. It's in Him that I can do all things. I'm totally content with being a little toe in the body where I work. Or in the church of that matter.

Paul addresses this in one of his letters to the church at Corinth. He says in 1 Corinthians 12:20-26:

But now indeed there are many members, yet one body. And the eye cannot say to the hand, "I have no need of you;" nor again the head to the feet, "I have no need of you." No, much rather, those members of the body which seem to be weaker are necessary. And those members of the body which we think to be less honorable, on these we bestow greater honor; and our unpresentable parts have greater modesty, but our presentable parts have no need. But God composed the body, having given greater honor to that part which lacks it, that there should be no schism in the body, but that the members should have the same care for one another. And if one member suffers, all the members suffer with it; or if one member is honored, all the members rejoice with it.

Paul, speaking about the church, reminds us that just because you are not what you believe to be the most "important" part, you are still part of the body and of more value than you realize. Everyone may want to be the head or the eyes, but then how will the body move? If everyone were the hands, how would the body breathe? My hands have never complained to me that they weren't feet—they're content being hands.

The same is true outside the church and in life in general. You don't have to have everything that everyone else has. You don't have to be the leader of some Fortune 500 company. You don't need to drive a Lamborghini (I hear they're very flammable anyway). You don't have to have the newest Jordan shoes. No matter what anyone tells you—even your boss. You're not a waste. You were bought with a price. And it's in that purchase price that you can find contentment.

🏋 WORDS TO WEIGH

1. What are some things the world considers "waste" that God considers valuable? Find Scriptures to support your list.

2. Conversely, what are some things the world considers valuable that God considers "waste"? Give Scriptures for each one.

3. What makes things valuable? How should our purchase price affect our lives? List a few verses that talk about our purchase price.

CH. 14
When the Waves Come

"I'm fine." "Another day in paradise." "Still chuggin' along." On a normal day, if you asked me how I was doing, you'd hear one of those responses. And 95% of the time, I wouldn't be lying to you. (Yes, I sometimes lie about how I am. I told you from the get-go, I'm just as flawed as the next guy). 95% of the time, I am fine. Nothing is going wrong. I feel like I'm making good progress in life. I'm just chugging along. Then one of those 5% days show up. That 5% is something else entirely.

They show up unexpectedly at the most random times, triggered by things that I have no control over. My train derails. The hamster falls off its wheel. Taking a breath becomes a fight with my lungs. My mind races. My heart stops. I feel trapped. I've lost count, even this month, how often it has happened to me. My life will be going completely normal and the next thing I know I'm back on the interstate in 2009, holding a young man as he dies. The joy in my life fades away and I start playing the "what if" game. You ever play that game? What if…I had driven a little faster? What if I had been up on the interstate like I should have been and as I had been every other Saturday morning rather than be in a pointless briefing? Then maybe I could have been there and prevented a wreck that would follow me around for the rest of my life. What if I had taken more medical classes? Maybe I could have done more to save him.

Grief is such an interesting dynamic in our lives. Everyone experiences it to varying degrees and others handle it better than others. At least it looks like they do anyway. You ever lose your car key? That's grief. Not to be compared with losing a loved one, but it is still grief. And you go through the same steps—just a little faster assuming you can find your keys. Failed a test? Been assaulted? Been cheated on? Car wreck? Lost a husband? Lost a baby? Unable to have babies? Been abused? Been abandoned? Kids leave the house and now you're empty nesters? You get the idea, because if you've been alive long enough to be reading this, you've been through something where grief has followed you.

I've had the opportunity to sit with numerous people when life decided to kick them in the face unexpectedly. Mike Tyson says, "Everyone has a plan until they get punched in the face." And that is very true especially when dealing with a loss. I say this in the context of someone who has lost more than his car keys—usually the loss of a loved one or some other extremely traumatic event. Somewhere in the haze that has filled their mind, the same question comes through: "What do I do now?" The answers I have found in my time hanging out with grief and the grieving are simple, but rarely easy.

"What do I do now?"

Nothing. Take time to do just that. Nothing. Your goal should be to just…be. A thousand questions will be running through your mind. Your brain is going to be going 1,000 miles per hour. You're going to want to go, go, go. In the beginning stages of grief, you need to just "be." Those questions can wait. Besides, we all know that there isn't an answer suitable to bring you any sense of calm now that your world has been turned upside down. So don't ask the question. Just…be.

I responded to a house where a young lady had come over to find her boyfriend had passed away unexpectedly from complications from diabetes. "What do I do now?" she asked me. "Nothing…we're just going to sit here." And we did. For the better part of three hours. We sat on her back porch watching the sunrise…just being.

It's normal.

What you are feeling is normal. Confusion, anger, hatred, etc. It's all a normal part of the grieving process. We went to a house once where a lady had woken to find her husband had passed away in his sleep. She ran out the front door and began beating on the side of every house in the neighborhood. It sounds crazy from the outside looking in, but that was normal.

I gave a death notification to a man whose brother had passed away in his car after years of being homeless. The man's reply: "Finally!" The brother had apparently been living for years with numerous health problems and would never take care of himself or accept any help from his family. Either way, that too was normal.

The only time the grieving process doesn't work is when we don't let it. And it starts to work when we understand that everything we feel, no matter how unnatural it is to us, is normal. You may experience feelings you have never felt in your entire life. Trust me—it's normal. You're not crazy—you're grieving.

Grief has a way of showing back up without warning.

We live by the Atlantic coast. The beach is a good stone's throw from my backyard. The boss lady and I love a good walk along the beach—especially when the sun is going down. It's so relaxing walking along the water's edge and feeling the water crash into your feet.

Our kids have become beach babies too. I remember the first time we took each one to the beach and dipped their little toes in the water. They weren't fans. But soon they got comfortable being around the water enough for us to let them stand on their own. They'd run and splash and be crazy little kids. Then when they weren't expecting it, a big wave would come along and knock them down.

That's how grief is—waves. Whatever happened might be fresh or have happened years ago. The waves of grief have a habit of just showing up and knocking you down. Nearly two decades after that accident, I will still be caught off guard by the memories. And you will be too depending on what you have experienced. For some it may be a man wearing a type of hat that a loved one used to wear. The smell of fresh bread might bring back memories of a grandmother. For the longest time, I couldn't drink sweet tea because it reminded me of my grandmother and the tea she used to make at home. Grief is like that.

Sometimes you can walk and let the waves crash at your feet. Sometimes the waves knock you over. I always try to remember who controls the sea (Mark 4:41). And in that, I find comfort.

Let's talk about it.

Cops are the worst at this. We loathe talking about what we have gone through. Especially to the non-cops. They just won't understand. I mean, how could you? You would have had to have been there with me—and you weren't. You didn't smell the gas, you didn't feel the blood running down my hands, you didn't see what I saw, feel what I felt, or hear what I heard. How could you possibly get what I'm feeling? Yet, I don't think that is the point of talking about it.

The point of talking about it is not about finding understanding or getting someone to understand, it's about acknowledging your struggle. No one will ever understand what you went through. Anyone who says they understand is lying. BUT—what can be understood is that you're in pain. And the right person with the right listening skills can, over time, help pick you up after the waves have taken you under. I found one just a few years ago.

In the winter of 2019, we were called to a local truck stop for an intoxicated female crying a bathroom stall. It was a Sunday morning around 9:00 a.m. when the call came. I had already made up my mind how this was going to go. She was probably a homeless alcoholic who was going to be a typical drunk we deal with on a regular basis. She probably spent the night getting hammered drunk and she was now in need of someone like me to take her to the Sheriff's Bed and Breakfast to sleep off the booze.

My partner and I got into the bathroom and got our first look at her. She was only wearing a tank top with shorts, and she was drunk. I mean d-r-u-n-k. She was holding on to a 40-ounce tallboy beer like her life depended on it. She had also been beaten halfway to Heaven. She had, as we say in the South, "toted a whoopin'." One eye was swollen almost shut, her lips were swollen, she had dried blood around her nose, her teeth were blood-stained, and her right wrist was broken. She was terrified that we were there and kept asking us to help her find her boyfriend. Who he was we didn't know. She wasn't the typical drunk I was expecting.

After the alcohol subsided, we were able to find out some of the details of what took place. She was being sex trafficked by a truck driver who worked for a Mexican cartel to which her family in Mexico owed a debt. She was to do whatever whenever the driver told her to, or a family member would be killed. That night, she fought back and paid the price. He beat her up then kicked her out of his truck. And for the next three or four hours, she walked around the parking lot in 40-degree weather in nothing but shorts and a tank top. No shoes. No jacket. The only help she found was a 40-ounce beer and an empty bathroom stall.

No matter what help we offered—she didn't want it. She just wanted to get back to the truck driver so her family would be okay. She let us take her to a local woman's shelter in the next city south of us. Five minutes after dropping her off, she ran out the back door. We never saw her again.

I had seen a lot of things in my career up to this point, but this one broke me. I got off that night in time for church services, but I couldn't make it through the door. I called my wife, and she met me in the parking lot. Through the tears I tried to explain what had happened. I'm not sure it really made any sense because I don't really remember what I said. I just remember crying and crying.

My first day in a therapist's office was quite the experience. I had never been before. I was doing great, or so I thought. I sat down on his big fluffy couch, and he hit me with the hardest question I had ever been asked. "So, what brings you in today?"

Y'all—I lost it. Nearly 20 years' worth of police experience came rushing out. I just sat on the couch and bawled my eyes out for 30 minutes. I couldn't talk. I just cried and cried and cried. Honestly, it was amazing. Best cry I had ever had. My time in his office was the first instance where I had actually talked to someone about my grief. It was really hard, but very rewarding.

He never told me that he understood what I was going through—because he didn't. He just listened and gave me some of the tips we just discussed. He told me I wasn't crazy. I wasn't alone. Everything I was feeling was normal. He encouraged healthy ways of coping with how I was feeling (walking, running, working out, creative arts, and…writing!). It has helped me tremendously. Though the waves still come, I remember the One who has the power to control them.

You may be going through a tough time right now. If not right now, you hang around long enough and a tough time will show up.

May I encourage you to speak with someone about it? Maybe your preacher, church leadership, a professional counselor, or your best friend. It is our job as Christians to "bear one another's burdens" (Galatians 6:2) and we can't do that if we don't know you have burdens that need bearing.

We have a saying around here: "Don't steal my blessing." I tried to give a lady money once when she brought us dinner one night because she found out we had lost someone close to us. "Don't steal my blessing," she quipped. She didn't do it for the money; she did it because she loved us. So many people can help walk with you through your grief if they are merely given the opportunity. Open up about it. Don't steal someone's blessing. Let them be the blessing when the waves come.

WORDS TO WEIGH

1. Grief is one of the most painful emotions we feel. Why do you think God allows us to feel it? What purpose might it serve in your life? List a few verses from Scripture that talk about grief and possible blessings.

2. What are some ways you individually can help someone who is in a deep state of grief? No cheating—list some things I didn't.

3. What are some ways the church as a whole can help a member in a deep state of grief? Is your congregation doing these? If not, get busy!

4. What Scriptures give you comfort in times of grief? List some verses that promise God cares and is listening and list some verses that provide hope.

CH. 15
SWAT School

Growing up in the 90s I watched *Cops* and every police movie I could get my hands on at Blockbuster. My favorite part, hands down, was when SWAT showed up. Special Weapons and Tactics. You knew business was about to get handled. It looked so cool! It was always a bunch of "I-love-the-gym" dudes wearing the coolest uniforms with the coolest tactical gadgets and carrying those fun guns. They'd line up in front of the door, the ram guy would destroy the door, the team would dump into the house, and chaos ensued. One SWAT guy would empty a magazine down a hallway while this other guy—apparently a Bruce Lee protégé—would be in the living room fighting off three bad guys with a spoon. I always thought that would be the greatest job ever. I didn't want to be president, a doctor, a lawyer (eww), or astronaut—I wanted join Door Kickers Inc. and catch the bad guys!

If you remember from the intro, I got my chance to go to SWAT school in 2012. SWAT school, at that time, was a weeklong course that taught you the basics of SWAT. You learned how to move as a team, the do's and don'ts of room clearing, when to go dynamic (fast), when to go in static (slow), how not to get in a lawsuit, legal considerations, CS gas exposure (that'll clear your sinuses), when to use CS gas, breaching, and how to deploy the light/sound diversionary devices (flash-bangs!). They had us rappel off a five-story building. We got to shoot the sub-machine guns with the fun switches. It was every little boy's dream that grew up in the 90's watching cop shows. The saying is "You're either SWAT, or you're not." But, before you got to do all the fun stuff, you must "shoot in" to the school.

The morning of day 1, you met with your potential class on the range. The instructors went over the range rules and then you had to shoot the standard qualifying course and get a score of 90%. It was a 30-round course from different ranges and positions where you were shooting targets that turn on the timer. To get that 90%, you had to score 270 out of 300. You got 10 points for center mass shots, 8 points for anything outside of center mass, and 0 points for missing. To ensure no one tried to cheat on the course, each shooter had an instructor standing directly behind them breathing on his neck. Oh, and you only got one chance to do it. The "cold-bore 90" was your first test in SWAT school. The pressure was intense. I almost forgot this part—only the top 25 shooters got in the school. That "90%" was the minimum required to get in. So, if you shot a 90% and 25 other people shot 91%—you didn't get in the school. If you didn't shoot 90%, you went home. Better luck next time! Do not pass go, do not collect $200. You got to take the long drive home, and everyone knew that you failed.

There I was standing 25 yards away when the first bullet was sent flying down range. The course only took a few minutes assuming there weren't any hangups. When the smoke cleared, my class dropped more than half the students. Thirty-five people showed up to the range, twenty went home. But not this guy. All those long days at the range doing all those shooting drills paid dividends. The countless reload drills, the drawing and re-holster and draw again, the thousands of rounds, the YouTube videos—they all paid off. Or it could have been my life as a kid also revolved around *Duck Hunt*. Either way, I smoked that course.

Then the fun began—SWAT school. They put us through scenario after scenario with someone new taking the leadership role. Everyone constantly rotated their positions in the unit. One scenario you were the shield guy, the next you were the breacher. This scenario you were holding a rifle. The next one, you held a shotgun. Sometimes you didn't get to be on entry at all— you got to be in the back holding the tools. It was boring but no less important than any other job. You might be the officer who went down or be the one who carried the injured officer. What was interesting is that the instructors didn't teach us how to handle every scenario—they taught us concepts on how to move and communicate together as one team and through our movements and communication, we would be able to overcome any scenario. They taught concepts like:

"A minimum of two people to a room." That means no one goes solo. This is a team effort. No hero stuff in SWAT. No one dives through a window to surprise the bad guy/guys. No "I saw this in a movie once and I think I can do it too" foolishness. We work together.

"Communicate with your team." If no one is talking, the team is probably wandering. The team leader needs to know what his/her team is doing, what they see, where they are going, etc. If I'm ready to dump into a room, I need to know if the guy behind me is ready. Do we need to slow down? Do we need to speed up? Is someone injured? Communication is one of the most vital parts of a team. When communication breaks down, mistakes are made. When mistakes are made, lives can be lost.

"Train. Train again. And when you're tired of training, train again." I can't tell you how many times I heard an instructor say, "That was good. Do it again." We would do movement after movement after movement. We would practice ejecting the magazine from the rifle then reloading it over and over. We would train when it was hot. When it was cold. We would train uphill, in the snow, both ways, with no shoes on—just like how Grandpa went to school. You get the idea. We trained. We trained because when the time comes to kick in someone's door at 3:00 a.m., we would be as prepared for the unexpected as we could be. When the unexpected showed up, we would be able to adapt. Amid the chaos, we would fall back on our training.

Isn't this exactly how the church should be? Be okay doing the less than glorious jobs? Be training, training, training? Be communicating with our church family rather than running out the door right after the final "Amen"? Shouldn't we be supporting each other? Let's take a gander at those ideas.

We all take on different jobs at different times. One day you are teaching a class and the next day you're cleaning up after a fellowship meal. I was on a mission trip in Honduras with Latin American Missions where one guy's sole job was to be at the door to the medical clinic and control the flow of people into the clinic. There was no glory in it. No award was given. But if he wasn't there to control the foot traffic, chaos ensued inside the clinic. No assignment in the church is more important than the other. Isn't that what Paul talked about in 1 Corinthians 12?

If the foot should say, "Because I am not a hand, I am not of the body," is it therefore not of the body? And if the ear should say, "Because I am not an eye, I am not part of the body," is it therefore not of the body? If the whole body were an eye, where would be the hearing? If the whole were hearing, where would be the smelling? But now God has set the members, each one of them, in the body just as He pleased. And if they were all one member, where would the body be? But now indeed there are many members, yet one body. And the eye cannot say to the hand, "I have no need of you" nor again the head to the feet, "I have no need of you." No, much rather, those members of the body which seem to be weaker are necessary (vs. 15-22).

Paul is saying that sometimes you're the guy standing in the background holding the tools while the rest of the team kicks in the door—and that's not a bad thing! And just like a SWAT team, when all the different parts work together as one cohesive unit, everything flows together.

What about when problems arise in and around the church? How are we, as a church, going to handle x, y, or z? You can't possibly prepare for every situation. I've been in the police world for over two decades. Every time I tell myself "I've seen it all," someone comes along and proves me wrong. But you know what your congregation can do to prepare for every situation? Embrace some simple concepts. I say "simple" in a "not complicated" kind of way. They aren't easy, per se, and they take a lot of practice.

No one goes alone. Don't try to face an obstacle/challenge in your life or in the church solo. If I had a penny for every time someone told me, "I've got some things to figure out myself and then…," I could afford that Lamborghini Huracan and almost fill up the tank (because these gas prices are out of control, right?). Some people—yours truly included—can be stubborn in asking for or receiving help. We feel it's a sign of weakness, don't we? I would never go into a house on a SWAT operation by myself, not because I'm weak, but because it is a lot safer when I have some SWAT dudes behind me. That way, if something happens to me, they have my back. If something happens to them, I have their back. That's what God intends for the church to do. If something happens to me, my church family will be there for me—and I should be there for them.

You can't do this life solo, and you especially can't do the Christian life alone. You weren't meant to either! Have you ever noticed that when Jesus sent out His disciples, He sent them in pairs (Mark 6:7)? He knew it was going to be hard. They were going out into the world without any money or food—just a staff. They would need each other! There were going to be times when one of them needed to be encouraged because even they didn't know what they were going to face. Neither do we! Paul had Silas (Acts 15:40). Elijah had Elisha (1 Kings 19:16). Life's problems are a lot easier to handle when you have those who are seeking wisdom and truth standing beside you. Isn't that what Solomon said in Ecclesiastes 4:9-12?

Two are better than one, Because they have a good reward for their labor. For if they fall, one will lift up his companion. But woe to him who is alone when he falls, For he has no one to help him up. Again, if two lie down together, they will keep warm; But how can one be warm alone? Though one may be overpowered by another, two can withstand him. And a threefold cord is not quickly broken.

We're going to keep open lines of communication with our congregation. This can be tough, I know. I'm not suggesting we air out all our dirty laundry to the church on Sunday morning after worship. I am suggesting that we take time to actually talk with our members, our deacons, our elders, our widows/widowers, our young people, and even those hormonal teenagers.

If you're a teenager, I challenge you to find an older member in your congregation and go have a sit-down conversation with them. Leave your phone in your pocket and go talk to them. Start to build a relationship with them—especially if they are a widow(er) (see James 1:27). Maybe offer to have a meal with them, mow their grass, wash their car, pick up their groceries, do their dishes, whatever! You can make a huge impact on their life and their faith, and so can they on yours!

Maybe you're older than a teen—find a young person to strike up a conversation. They can be gross, smelly, and weird—I get it. I worked in the school system for some years; I got it! Here is a pro tip. To get to a young person's heart, you don't go through his brain, you go through his stomach! Bring food. We have the sweetest ladies in our congregation who keep gummy candy and Goldfish by their seats. After services, the kids flock to them to get some snacks. These ladies have them figured out—and every kid loves them. Teens aren't much different; they love food.

Maybe you invite the preacher out to lunch after services. Perhaps your family writes individualized "thank you" cards to your elders and deacons. You know what happens when you build these relationships by communicating with other members of your congregation? You build trust that they know you care for them and they care for you. When you have that trust established and life's Mike Tyson punches you in the schnoz, you have people that you feel comfortable to lean on for support.

I've been to congregations where people can't get out of the building fast enough after the last "amen" is spoken. I open my eyes, and half the people are gone. Zero effort is used to communicate with other members of the church. When a congregation doesn't communicate, the members begin to wander. Jesus' ministry was so effective because He was so personal with those around Him. He took time to listen to people, talk with people, eat with people, feed people, and love people. The Gospel accounts are overflowing with examples of how you and I can be better to those around us.

We're going to train, train, and train some more. Then when we're tired of training, we're going to train more. God gave those instructions to the Israelites in Deuteronomy 11:18-21.

> *Therefore you shall lay up these words of Mine in your heart and in your soul, and bind them as a sign on your hand, and they shall be as frontlets between your eyes. You shall teach them to your children, speaking of them when you sit in your house, when you walk by the way, when you lie down, and when*

> *you rise up. And you shall write them on the doorposts of your house and on your gates, that your days and the days of your children may be multiplied in the land of which the Lord swore to your fathers to give them, like the days of the heavens above.*

You know what happened when they neglected their training? They slipped away. You see it time and time again throughout the Old Testament. Moses was only on the mountain for 40 days before the Israelites abandoned God and made a golden calf to worship (Exodus 32). They had just witnessed everything that took place in Egypt and in just over a month without Moses, they are knee deep in idol worship. The people didn't believe they could take Canaan after 10 of the 12 spies claimed it couldn't be done (Numbers 13). They complained against God and Moses after being brought out of the slavery of Egypt (Numbers 21) which resulted in God sending snakes into the camp. You don't have to read far into each book of the Old Testament to find another example.

That is what happens when you don't train—you get sloppy in your faith. You can tell when it's been some time since our last SWAT training session. People start making mistakes they wouldn't have made. The same thing happens when you skip out on your Bible study, worship, etc.—you get sloppy in your faith. You start to forget the things written down for our comfort and admonition (Romans 15:4). It doesn't take long to end up on the mountainside worshiping a golden calf. You must keep up with your training.

We're going to do more than attend than our midweek Bible studies and Sunday school lessons. Start looking outside your congregation at extra opportunities to further your faith. Marriage seminars, youth rallies, mission trips, lectureships—you name it, we're going. Anything where I can get a mustard seed of instruction that can help me help people with their faith—I'm in.

I attended some classes at Polishing the Pulpit (PolishingThePulpit.com) once where we were split into groups and each group given a problem one church faced. We were given a few minutes to discuss the problem and come up with a way to biblically address it. You learn what the leadership there did and what they learned from the experience. We covered topics like theft, adultery, addiction, false doctrines, etc. It really makes you think! In the police world, we call this type of training a "debrief."

Perhaps we take our family (even the smelly teens) to a family camp like Legacy Family Camp East (LegacyFamilyCampEast.com). Nearly a week of God-centered and family-focused lessons and activities with the intent to strengthen our homes. Time away from the hustle and bustle of our daily lives to bring us closer together.

The whole point of this is to try to make us better Christians so we can then be better Christians to someone else. Maybe you'd take something away from a family retreat that could help a dad who is struggling. Perhaps you could be the difference in a young person's life because you attended a youth rally. You have to train, train, train because when the spiritual bullets start flying, you revert back to your training. If your training is subpar or just average, so will be your response.

Picture this: You stop in your local gas station for a quick snack. You're debating between that bag of peanut M&M's and the tropical fruit Skittles. Well, you love God so you grab the M&M's. But as you turn to pay the cashier, some murderer who was just in a vehicle pursuit with the police comes running into the store and takes you and the cashier hostage. Who do you want coming to help you? The SWAT team that trains often, keeps their gear sharp, and take their job seriously? Or would you be okay with the team filled with guys who show up to training unless one of their kids has a baseball game, and if they actually show up, they're usually asleep or playing on their phone? Who do you really want to come save you? When your life is falling apart and you need some assurance that God hasn't left you, who do you want to give you that assurance? The one who is a Christian on more than just Sunday morning or the one who honors God with their lips, but their heart is far from Him (Matthew 15:8)?

Police officers often say they have one goal each shift: to make it home. We as Christians have that same goal, don't we? To make it Home? To Heaven? To hear our Savior say, "Well done, good and faithful servant"? Making it home—whether you are a police officer or a Christian—doesn't happen by accident. You will never accidentally find yourself home in Heaven. You must be intentional about seeking wisdom and truth. It takes time, practice, sacrifice, and teamwork. Being a Christian seeking wisdom and truth is difficult and the way narrow. Not everyone will do it—in fact, most won't (Matthew 7:13-14). But the peace and the joy it brings are beyond comprehension. Romans 8:18 says, "For I consider that the sufferings of this present time are not worthy to be compared to the glory that will be revealed in us." That means seeking wisdom and truth will be worth it!

"He who is not with Me is against Me, and he who does not gather with Me scatters abroad." (Matthew 12:30). That's Jesus' way of saying that you're either *Seeking Wisdom and Truth*, or you're not.

So now it's your turn to stand on the firing line. You get to choose what you're going to do with your life. You don't get three magazines loaded with bullets—you only get one shot. One chance to hit the mark. One pull of the trigger. That's all you get in this life. But when your one shot is done and the smoke clears, what will Jesus see? Will He see that you spent your life *Seeking Wisdom and Truth*? After all, you're either *SWAT* or you're not.

WORDS TO WEIGH

1. Why is so difficult to ask for help? Why do we (yours truly included) feel like we must handle everything by ourselves? Find two verses that discuss what we should do instead.

2. What are some things that cause communication to break down (a) in the home and (b) in the church?

3. What are your talents? How can you use your gifts and strengths to benefit the body of Christ whether you are a foot, a head, or an eye? Be specific with ways!

4. List some New Testament verses about training and the benefits it brings.

5. Do police really like donuts?

   I'll answer this one for you at no extra charge. Yes. Yes, we do! Here is your homework—go buy your local Police Department/Sheriff's Office some donuts. They'll appreciate it, I promise. "What about the fire department?" you ask. Ya, anyway...just buy the cops donuts. The fire department will be fine without them.

About the Author

Jon Zirpolo is a present-day superhero to his wife of over 15 years and their three boys, as well as on the streets of Richmond Hill, Georgia. He spends his days fighting crime and walking by faith as a law enforcement officer. As a LEO for over 20 years, he has seen many things that would make most run for the hills. His experiences have tried and shaped his faith, which led to his desire to share the Word of God with others.

When he's not patrolling, he loves spending time with his family and his retired K9 partner Milan, especially at the beach. Jon and his family worship at Richmond Hill church of Christ.

Jon is an occasional runner and a self-proclaimed YouTube mechanic. He is also a speaker and often holds seminars on the internet and its dangers.

www.ingramcontent.com/pod-product-compliance
Lightning Source LLC
LaVergne TN
LVHW010113280226
832808LV00044B/1006